50 Years – 50 Lessons

A Middle-Aged Man's Suggestions for
Not Fecking Things Up – Now and in
Later Life!

50 Years – 50 Lessons

A Middle-Aged Man's Suggestions for
Not Fecking Things Up – Now and in
Later Life!

Fergal Barr

IFF
BOOKS

Winchester, UK
Washington, USA

JOHN HUNT PUBLISHING

First published by iff Books, 2022
iff Books is an imprint of John Hunt Publishing Ltd., No. 3 East Street, Alresford,
Hampshire SO24 9EE, UK
office@jhpbooks.com
www.johnhuntpublishing.com
www.iff-books.com

For distributor details and how to order please visit the 'Ordering' section on our website.

ISBN: 978 1 80341 283 2
978 1 80341 284 9 (ebook)
Library of Congress Control Number: 2022910228

A CIP catalogue record for this book is available from the British Library.

Design: Lapiz Digital Services

UK: Printed and bound by CPI Group (UK) Ltd, Croydon, CR0 4YY
Printed in North America by CPI GPS partners

We operate a distinctive and ethical publishing philosophy in
all areas of our business, from our global network of authors to
production and worldwide distribution.

Contents

Dedication

To my three children – Michaela, Laya, and Josh – and my two beautiful grandchildren – Gerry, and Phoebe, who give me reason to get up every day.

To my parents – Hugh and Eilis – they tried their best and for that I am grateful.

To Aine, Riona and Aoibhín – they brought many new lessons at a time when I probably needed them.

To all those that endeavour to be a better version of themselves every day.

To those who take time to think before they decide.

Introduction

It will probably sound a bit cliched, but life did seem a little bit easier when I was growing up in the '80s. In many ways the expectations were the same – go to school, and when you finish get a job, or if not go on to college or university. And then you'd be expected to find a 'someone', settle down, start a family, and live happily ever after.

In most respects I followed this – although the 'someone' came after school, followed by starting a family and then settling down before going to university. When I finished school, I had no intention of going back into education, but needs must and all that.

I fell into youth work as a career by 'accident' and if I wanted to succeed, I had to get the piece of paper that would allow me to apply for certain jobs and get better paid essentially. During this time, I got married and had a young family, and so I needed to ensure money was coming in – I was a father and husband with responsibilities!

The next ten years, give or take a few months, played out as 'normal'; more children followed, but then my wife and I split up and I had to start over again – this time on my own – find a new house, make it 'liveable' for my children staying over, continue to work, make ends meet, and find a new 'someone' to share my life with. No pressure!

I made the house 'liveable', continued to work (albeit freelancing on quite a few occasions), and of course my kids grew up. I'm now at the grandfather stage, and still without the 'someone' new in my life although not always. I can't say I'm unhappy, though – I've had a decent life, I'm grateful for all the opportunities presented to me and those I have managed to create. I have managed to stay solvent even in some difficult moments, and I'm still here!

All of this has happened in what feels like a blink of an eye. It really does feel like it's no time since I was coming home from school and heading out to the front green to play football. When I was younger, this was all I cared about. I just wanted to play football and even though I've clocked up more than half a century I still play, at least twice a week, at the time of writing.

My needs and expectations have of course changed but it's with this in mind that I have put pen to paper. As we grow up, we are all socialised into a world in which there are all manner of expectations, values and beliefs imposed upon us. Even if they're not forced on us as such, they are there, often lurking in the background, often oblivious to us and perhaps without our even asking why.

When I was growing up, and 'evolving' as a human – in my 20s, 30s, and 40s – it was only through the trial and error of my own lived experience, my natural curiosity, my own desire to learn and understand why things are the way they are, my regular questioning of that which I didn't understand and my willingness to put aside my own convictions, sometimes begrudgingly, that I began to realise that all those expectations, values and beliefs imposed upon us don't necessarily have to be how we should live our lives.

To say the last few years have been fairly momentous is an understatement – BREXIT, Covid, BLM (Black Lives Matter), Trump, the clamp-down in Hong Kong, Capitol Hill insurrection, anti-Maskers/'Vaxxers', Trucker Protests in Canada, the 'exodus' from Central America to the US and also from Africa into Europe, Climate Change, the growth of populism and nationalism, sports stars taking the knee, the US pulling out of Afghanistan as well as abandoning the Syrian Kurds, the collapse of the Iran Nuclear Deal, the continued persecution of Uyghurs in China, and the invasion of Ukraine by Russia (at the time of writing) and the cost of living crisis, are just some of the headline events among many in a tumultuous period in human history.

If you were to follow news on a regular basis, whether through your TV, radio, tablet, laptop, newspaper, or phone, or a combination of any of these, you'd be forgiven for thinking that the world is on the verge of self-destruction or that we're headed for a date in the not too-distant future where many of the pressures on the world will coalesce and we'll tip over into some post-apocalyptic state.

Recently, a 1970s sustainability paper by Gaya Hetherington predicting the collapse of civilisation in 2040 has gained traction among those looking for evidence of same, although she herself is at pains to point out it isn't inevitable and if we change our ways, we can indeed create a different reality.

All of us have a collective responsibility to try and ensure that we play our part in trying to minimise the potential for reaching any kind of tipping point, be that being more aware of and active towards things like climate change or even just nurturing and encouraging greater levels of kindness and compassion to those not only around us but the more needy.

Having clocked up a half-century in Earth years, I guess I've reached some kind of 'mid-way point', in that I'm closer now to 60 than 40, and thus whilst I still consider myself relatively young, as does society at large, I am (as what we might say in Northern Ireland) 'no spring chicken' and therefore arguably my best days are behind me. The reality is that as we get older, we are more vulnerable to all sorts of ailments, our bodies begin to age, we creek a bit more, but that said, we tend to be (or at least should be) a little wiser, more mature, a little less re-active, possess greater perspective and can take a 'helicopter view' on things.

Even as a grandfather now, I approach my grandchildren in a different way than I did when I was parenting my own children – I'm more chilled, more relaxed, less stressed, less demanding, I have tailored my expectations, I have more insight into how things are and how I can be more pragmatic and realistic, and more kind, caring and compassionate.

It's with that in mind that I wanted to share lessons I have picked up over my lifetime because if I can share my learning with others and prevent anyone making the same mistakes I have made, then I will have achieved something, a kind of legacy of sorts.

I appreciate that everyone has to live their own life, make their own mistakes and experience their own highs and lows in order to become the person they are and I would never want to block that natural learning process for anyone, but I also wish that I had come to some of the conclusions that are borne out in this book quicker than I have done, as that would have made life a little more smooth.

Unlike many other books, my intention is not to tell you how to change, live or behave, but rather share with you some of the lessons I have learned, and if that helps to influence, shape, mould or inform how you to move forward more positively, then I will be happy with that.

I wish you good health and good fortune on your own respective journey.

Fergal Barr

Your beliefs don't make you a better person, your behaviour does.
Unknown

1. In the search for meaning, ultimately it comes down to this – most of it doesn't really matter so just enjoy

My goal is not to be better than anyone else, but to be better than I used to be.
Dr Wayne W. Dyer

The last few years have been a period of reflection for me – nothing startling or amazing about that I guess, everyone does it I assume at some point – short periods, long periods. I hit 50 in May '21 – nothing startling or amazing about that either but my kids have grown up (and still growing up as it turns out), I now have two grandchildren and in recent years, I've had periods of unemployment and working freelance which have given me time to reflect, consider, contemplate, wonder, think, worry and... read a lot too.

What conclusion have I reached? A few in fact but here's the main one which I'll offer now because any of you reading this will want to know if you are still deciding whether to read on. I'm no different but if you want to know why I have reached the following conclusion that I am about to share with you, then you'll have to read through. If you decide not to, then just take a moment or two to consider what you're about to read in the next paragraph.

Like you I am merely one person in a population of more than seven billion people on a large planet (very small in planetary terms) which is in a galaxy known to us as the Milky Way (across an infinite universe) where 'some of its stars are almost as old as the universe (more than 13 billion years old) [and] within our galaxy lie 200 to 400 billion stars... in our galaxy lies our sun, a teenager at a mere 4.57 billion years old'[1] and in terms of our evolution, civilisation has been around since about 11.59 p.m. on the world evolutionary clock.

When all is said and done, most of what we give a damn about isn't really worth giving a damn about and all I can really give a damn about is those closest to me because ultimately when we're gone, we're gone, it's over, done with, kaput – and as we all know too well, life is precious, life is vulnerable – in all of our pomp and glory one minute yet pushing up daisies or occupying an urn the next.

So let me begin by first telling you where I'm coming from which might help to contextualise my main conclusion a little. I'm a youth worker by profession (or as I prefer to say by trade) and have now managed to amass more than 30 years in youth work – 27 of those professionally qualified (at the time of writing) from Ulster University or the University of Ulster as it was back then. I still can't get used to that 'enormous' rebrand!

For the first 20 years of my life religion played a significant part in my life. I was raised in the Roman Cathartic... oops, sorry, the Roman Catholic tradition and would have described myself as a 'right-wing conservative Catholic' fuelled by a full-on commitment to the 'rules of the club' – yip, I even kept my confirmation pledge to not drink alcohol till I was 18.

Such commitment to said rules can only mean one thing – I was probably a little hard to bear at times, although my parents where mightily proud of me – well having a picture of Pope John Paul II on your bedroom door is likely to make any Catholic parents proud. Mind you, I wasn't all good – as the only one who looked over the age of 18 when I was in my mid-teens, I was the one going into the off-licence for my friends – they'd get drunk and I'd be around to look after them. Imagine buying alcohol from an off-licence that you're not going to drink!

Anyhow, fast forward to the present and I have moved from one end of the spectrum to the other. I simply questioned, critiqued, and challenged many of the beliefs I had grown up with (even cherished) and eventually concluded, that whilst religion did instil in me many important values, I simply didn't need religion of any kind to guide me on how to live my life – in fact the opposite, it was making me self-righteous and that's not a very admirable quality. After all, if you are going to be a member 'of the club' you need to stick to the rules – you just can't cherry-pick, right? Tut, tut, these part-time Catholics – flip me!

The passing years have been informed by a growing commitment to trying to live my life in as humane a way as possible. And what have I learned? Many things of course but not least of all that the more I know the more I don't know but that's quite abstract so let me try and be a little more specific.

I'm anything but perfect (deep down I always knew that anyway) but as a full practising member of the club I had God on my side and thus I must be right, right? WRONG! I've made mistakes, many – small, medium and those that have been indelibly left with two size 9 shoe prints.

In realising I'm far from perfect and having accepted my human side (and still accepting it by the way) but having stopped long ago (as it so happens) trying to strive for perfection I have come to embrace a number of mottos that I try to live by.

My most common motto is, or rather was (now replaced with *it is what it is*), is *there's always someone worse off than you* which is designed to remind me that when I think things are bad, they're not as bad as they could be and thus the need for a little humility is necessary.

Humour is the shortest distance between people is another one (laughter is a language we all share and a currency we can exchange no matter how poor we are) and you can read more on this further in Lesson 36.

I truly believe that humour, and music, is a cure-all for many of society's ills (but that's another conversation) – no wonder that in certain parts of the world 'they' ban music – the power of it is so well known. And no wonder that humour, especially satire and irony is often frowned upon by authority not to mention certain governments.

These mottos are designed to illustrate how I wanted to live my life (and still do) and in doing so, acknowledging that I'm anything but perfect but also recognising that I've been very lucky in my life – no major traumas of any kind – my health is generally good (I can't swim far and I'm certainly not marathon material, but my health is decent). Bereavement has never really been visited upon me, nor has life-changing events or life-defining challenges – compared to some people that I know, none – I have been very lucky! I am grateful!

Now, that's not to say there haven't been challenges – finding consistent work in my chosen profession over the last few years has proven more and more difficult. I also went through divorce and whilst it wasn't without its challenges, I emerged stronger for it – a lot less wealthy mind you (financially speaking), not that I was ever really that wealthy.

Perhaps on paper it might have appeared so but then 2008 came – Lehman Bros-housing-crash-divorce and voila, any wealth accrued, perceived or otherwise – gone! The reality is that if I don't find 'X' number of pounds over the next decade or so I might be bunking in with my kids – assuming in this current climate they have no intentions of moving back in with me!

So, I have been quite lucky in many respects – essentially no meaningful wealth but as it stands, enough to live on day-by-day which (it can be said) is much more than for millions worldwide.

There has of course been a number of challenges – some of those relationships closest to me in recent years have led to much soul-searching, reflection and contemplation – stressful at times but nothing that compares with someone who has just received or is coming to terms with the news of a terminal illness, for example.

I fully appreciate what I have even when there are challenges. And it's with this in mind I come back to my opening point about what's really important – an enforced period of unemployment/ freelance did provide me with time (time that wasn't available when I was busy) and thus I had the opportunity to look at things differently.

I never was (nor am I now) someone that is materialistic – I have a notion of what I can only describe as a 'decluttering process' that leads me to the idea of living (a very simple existence) out of an old VW Camper (we had one when we were younger and so I have terribly fond memories of them) and not being part of the multiple house-owning communities that have emerged with such frequency in the last number of decades, primarily in Western democracies I might add.

In many ways most of us got in at the wrong time and bought into the dream that has become a bit of a nightmare in many respects. When you think about it, who honestly would agree to pay back £2.50 for every £1 borrowed over 20 years with no guarantee you'd own anything at the end of it? Ludicrous really but many of us have done so (or similar), perhaps paying back even more. This was the last deal I got on a mortgage – not very attractive but beggars can't be choosers.

I was talking to a friend some time ago – he bought his dream house in County Donegal, Ireland, several years ago – think he mentioned a mortgage of €100, 000 or more only to discover that there were problems with the materials used to build it, and now? Well, a home that's literally crumbling but a mortgage he still has with the bank on a property he can't live in or get shot of.

You might have heard about this – MICA blocks – just search for it online and you'll get the story. When he told me of the story at the time, he didn't know what was behind it, now it's clear but he like many others, bought into the housing dream – my own situation is nothing compared to his, but essentially lumbered by debt which obliges me to be in work continuously, but hey, *it is what it is*, no point getting angry about it, right?

In terms of reflecting on events I have considered many important questions in recent times – not (the) *what is the meaning of life* type but more so where am I going now (after a generation in youth work), what am I looking to achieve, what should I be focusing on, how best can I apply myself, how should I live my life from now on and so on and so on.

And whilst my periods of unemployment have helped to create the context for such reflection it was a very tragic event in Buncrana, Co. Donegal, in 2016, when five members of one family lost their lives (when their car slid off a pier) that brought sharply into focus how easily life can be lost – the nature and circumstances were particularly heartbreaking.

In the same year when many celebrities we knew of (but didn't actually know in person), i.e., David Bowie, Prince, George Michael et al., also passed, seemingly very suddenly, and when the suffering and inhumanity of what was going on in Syria and other parts of the world is interspersed with headline grabbing stories that was Paris, Brussels, Ankara, Baghdad, Nice and so on, it becomes clearer that life is precious, yet so immensely vulnerable. Here in full glory one moment, obituaries the next. The irony is that humanity is experiencing a more peaceful time in its history than at any other time but with rolling media it just doesn't seem like it or feel like it for that matter.

The last few years have brought to the fore a time to stop, take stock and to think, Covid and BLM among them of course; and this also presented opportunities to do other things that also by circumstance might not have happened, i.e., making time to pick up my mother, for example, on Friday's for her to go shopping, lifting my father on Saturday's to go visit his sister – things that might have been a duty or chore or out of necessity but have become moments to enjoy, savour, embrace and make time for and build memories around as they entered their most senior of years but at a time when ill-health had also become a feature of their life. At the time of writing, both have become frailer in part because Parkinson's and Dementia has now become a factor in their lives and so, time is even more precious.

A few years back I had found someone to share my life with and to be in the company of her immediate and wider family whilst entering a new phase in my relationship with my own children as they are now 'all grown up' as well as becoming a grandparent, not once but twice, has also helped to inform my wider reflection on life's priorities.

I now have a much greater appreciation of these moments, so much so that at no point in my own life have I become clearer nor had a stronger desire to give of myself to family than now. That's not to say I didn't in the past but now I have a much greater appreciation of what is truly important.

I mentioned that I used to pick my mother up to go shopping on Friday mornings and on many occasions, I had 'brunch' with her – lunch for her, breakfast for me as she was always up from about 8 a.m. whilst I was sometimes only getting out of my bed to go lift her. In the restaurant that we used to go into a lot of elderly patrons used to frequent and it's during this time, when I was a spritely 40+, I also got to see and hear at first hand, about some of the challenges and conversations that these fine upstanding elderly patrons have or had. And it was during this time I also got a sense of my own mortality. And thus, began to also realise the need to appreciate the time we have on this spinning ball of dust and gas.

Now, in terms of this period of reflection I'm not going to sit here and pretend I don't get cranky, frustrated and impatient with things, situations or people (except when I'm playing indoor football on Tuesday and Thursday nights – that doesn't count, we're allowed to be Neanderthal-like then) but I now appreciate much more the importance that we often afford to

13

things that require certain energies – namely negative, which are also often misplaced and confused with asserting our identity, or at least a facet of it. When someone jumps the queue, looks at us in the 'wrong way' or treats us in a way we don't feel demonstrates respect, there is a tendency to give out or react in a particular way.

I have reached a kind of conclusion that much of what we 'stress' over (and I appreciate that stress has multiple meanings for everyone) is ultimately, just not that important anymore. I have two two-seater sofas at home and most of the time they are adorned by two throws (don't worry I do wash them from time to time) with the words, 'God grant me the serenity to accept the things I cannot change, courage to change the things I can and wisdom to know the difference'. I know this contrasts with my earlier assertion about religion but it's the essence of the words that I love.

It reminds me of one of my other mottos, 'it doesn't matter what you say, people will talk about you anyway' so try not to waste too much energy, if any at all, on negativity (especially that of others) because there are some things that you won't be able to change and knowing the difference between what you can and can't change will have much more of a positive outcome for your daily existence.

Now that's not to say you should give up on taking a stand against injustice, unfairness, inequality, violence and so on but as a good friend of mine once said, 'pick your fights' or rather, know whom or what to engage and at which moment to do so.

You see, there comes a point in life when you realise in which direction you should channel your energies. When I was younger, I wanted to (and genuinely believed I could) change the world – of course that was more a reflection of my perception of the world, my faith in human capacity, not least of all my own and somehow my belief that if everyone tried to live like I lived we'd all be much better off – yeah, I know, tell me about it, how naive was I, or rather how self-righteous was I about my own way of living?

But it was that naivety that allowed me to believe in change, a belief that change was always possible if we'd only try hard enough. That fundamental belief of creating change hasn't changed, I'm just much more realistic about it and what it takes to create change and how we need to look at things differently, from new perspectives, if we are to bring about change and that change begins in our minds.

The world needs more people like me back in my teens (without the self-righteousness of course), not 'tainted' or tempered by experience but driven by an unquestionable sense of justice and belief, with the energy to fight, to challenge, to uphold the values that make humanity great, yet we also need those who provide something equally as important – people to create space and time and love, care and compassion – not in some kind of spiritual guru and priestly fashion but just in a manner that helps to create tranquillity, understanding and calmness.

During my 'sabbatical' (that's code for previous bouts of unemployment and freelancing), I learned to read a lot and have continued to do so. The books I read are not novels – more so, I focus on books that explore subjects such as how does the brain work, how does humanity operate, the challenges of the future, trying to live a more peaceful and harmonious existence and so on – needless to say it poses profound questions, not the 'will Liverpool ever win the Premier League title (again)' kind of question, but those that throw into doubt assumptions we make about our current existence and at what cost have we reached the point we're now at.

As I've pointed out earlier, most of what we give a damn about isn't really worth giving a damn about and so it's with this in mind that I have come to consider the question of legacy – I think about this in a broader context, a context where in certain parts of the world indiscriminate conflict exists alongside absolute poverty, homelessness, disease, corruption, torture and so on (you can make your own list). And I think to myself, what can I do to try and change that – have I got the power to do something about it, the resources even and most importantly the desire and passion?

Well, yes is the simple answer. Back in 2001 I took a former employer to an Industrial Tribunal and won a test case (I represented myself) and changed employment law in Northern Ireland *forever* (had to add forever for dramatic effect even if it is true) and therefore any of us at a given moment can effect change when driven to do so but of course it takes more than just energy, drive and belief – many other factors come into play, some of them we have no control over, but our own energy can generate other energies in multiple ways.

It's when I think of this question about change and the capacity to bring about change I think about change makers – Cameron, Blair, Trump, Putin – nah, only kidding, change makers of an entirely different kind they are but that's for another day – I think of the obvious ones: Gandhi, Luther King, Mandela, Tutu, Jesus, etc., (etc. is code for a momentary lapse of memory where I can't think of any more names) and it's then that I begin to consider what is it I want to achieve in my remaining days and what will be my message that forms part (if not all) of my legacy.

The concept of legacy is quite an interesting one in many respects – when we think of legacy, we tend to think of it in terms of achievements and often this is measured in physical or other kinds of materialistic ways or at least it certainly feels like that in our twenty-first-century Westernised culture.

Leaving a sum of money or a property or putting down a marker that helped create change or helped to influence the lives of others is also among the notions we have around legacy. In my role as a youth worker I have always said that we are defined by our actions and what I mean by that is this: the message we leave behind in our work with young people, the impression(s) we leave – of course we can say and do things that we don't necessarily mean, or subscribe to but sometimes we only get one shot at things and if we screw up it can be very hard to undo what is done – and thus the message we leave behind can be of much greater significance.

Over the years I have bumped into young people I have worked with, and they recite key moments in their lives where I exercised influence or played a significant role at a particular moment which made a difference in their lives.

Many years ago, one young person approached me in a bar one evening to double check it was me and then to let me know that the DJ course I organised (many years before that again) in which he had enrolled started his career in DJing, and he wanted to thank me.

This is not to take away from other factors at work, at least in this instance, i.e., as Youth Workers our general commitment to provide youth services, or his mother registering him (and his cousins so they would be busy during the summer holidays), or his decision to take part and give lots of energy to it at the time.

That said, to have someone come up and offer me their story and how I influenced their life is not only wonderful to hear but just simply reassuring that my efforts were not in vain and that the time and energy invested had been worth it.

Some years ago, whilst on a trip to Belgrade for a planning meeting, I flew to Budapest where my colleagues and I were picked up and taken by minibus on a five-hour drive. I noticed our driver looked a little tired (but thought perhaps he always looks like this) and as I took my place in the front seat I thought, need to keep an eye here – not easy when you've been travelling most of the day and you're leaving on a 5-hour journey at 10 p.m. But I did, and thankfully so, because for one moment he dozed off (only for a second) and I asked him if he was, okay?

He replied that he was whilst trying to impress upon me that he had just been looking at something out the window.

It was only further on in the journey at about 70 miles an hour and inches from hitting the car in front and going off the motorway that I gently (in what might constitute a loudish but eloquently abrupt fashion) reminded the driver he might want to 'watch out for the car in front' (or words to that effect).

In a sense that was a legacy moment – effectively I had saved both the driver and I, not to mention the other 7 passengers in the back from death or serious injury (none of whom would have known shit as they were all sleeping). Yip, it was like that moment from Father Ted when Ted, Dougal and Jack have been driving all night whilst asleep. My colleague from Estonia who was travelling with me knew nothing of what had happened till we arrived at our hostel – still waiting on that beer for saving her life!

I tell that story not by way of saying, hey look, I saved the lives of others but rather as part of our legacy which isn't necessarily about materialism – monetary value, physical pleasure or otherwise, but rather how our actions can have positive outcomes in the lives of others – I also tell it because I see the 'funny' side of it and reminds me of my own NDE (Near Death Experience) when falling asleep at the wheel on my way home from Belfast one evening many years ago and also, how sometimes we are meant to stay alive.

At this time of my life the issue of legacy is one which is driven by desire, passion and not least of all, motivation. Much of my motivation is about savouring the experience, enjoying the moment and just being free in that moment – be that a walk through a busy city centre when all about me is rushing to and from the next meeting, appointment or victory; people-watching over a nice cuppa; enjoying a pint and a book on a sunny day; or still 'living out' some childhood dreams at indoor football twice a week, my motivation tends to revolve around the experience, the enjoyment I get from what I'm doing and just being in that moment, i.e., being present.

Whilst I now take time to enjoy these moments more than I ever did, particularly as childhood was about discovery and youth was about exploration followed by my 20s and 30s which was dominated by parenting and all the challenges and pressures that that brings, my 40s was (as is my 50s even more so) about savouring the moments and being free to choose, which also means rather than trying to fit somewhere into the fast lane and being part of the conveyor belt of life, I can still create change, make things more simple, not complicate life (because it tends to be complicated enough already and we humans seem committed to making it more complicated) but aspiring to a more simple life, a life where I get to choose the passions I want to pursue.

The fabulous car, the exclusive house, the annual holiday in the sun and so on are not my priorities but rather my passions for humour (and promoting and sharing my own *Humour is Serious Business* programme); music (listening to it more and more, creating an album of covers of favourite songs and even a spot of DJing); promoting international youth work (continuing to provide international learning opportunities to local youth workers as I have done for over 14 years); publishing a second book of poetry and still trying to convince the Ulster University of the merits of a PhD proposal on the impact of international youth work on post-conflict societies – these are a mix of recent and current passions – they don't pay much in terms of returns, financially-speaking, but they are my passions.

You see, I've come to a conclusion (another one I hear you say) that most decisions, answers and responses to questions, challenges and problems are not informed by logic, common sense or a desire to ease the burden and stress on our daily lives but are determined by personality – and of course personality is made up of emotions, values, belief, ideology, mood, context and so on. And whilst most of us would probably say we are committed to things like inclusion, equality and human rights, we are a species that is governed by experience, bias, prejudice, wants, needs and things that are close and personal to us.

I'm not for one second suggesting that this is bad because we can't function without any of these, but alongside our assumptions, the decisions we make are ultimately at the whim of all those things mentioned, thus raising questions of whether or not there can be truly fairness, justice and equality for anyone never mind everyone.

I guess what I'm saying is that we all recognise the need to aspire to fairness, justice and equality and we endeavour to try and achieve this, but can we truly be this all the time?

There are many great acts of kindness, care, love, and compassion – life is short (relatively speaking of course) and can be so beautiful – but we live in a world where most of the decisions that affect us are made by other individuals who (like us), are subject to all the various influences I have already mentioned.

When I sit back now and think what my priorities are (apart from my passions), I think about my legacy and the message(s) I want to leave behind; I don't really have any money, so it must be messages.

My focus now is on key messages, messages about values and principles, ideals that we hold dear, ways in which we live or have lived our lives, commitments to being true to ourselves, a passion for things we care about, a desire for a more peaceful and calm existence, being innovative and creative when we can or when is necessary, an aspiration that helps me to keep believing in my own capacity to contribute positively in the lives of those I come into contact with, or help nurture dreams that enable me to look into the future with hope, and a belief that we can truly be more than we ever imagined.

I am far from perfect but of course no one is in any case and what is perfect anyway? I am no more right than anyone else (we all believe we are right of course because that's what gives us our values and beliefs) but I have clear ideas on how I should live and if invited by others to share, I will be happy to share them, but be careful when inviting me to do so.

I have reached that point where I am now committed to achieving a state of 'contentment' rather than pursuing happiness – pursuing happiness is fine but all too often can lead only to disappointment. The search for happiness can be endless and is always being redefined in many ways or is merely relative to your own circumstance but I smile and laugh when life invites me. I say more on this later in lessons on contentment and also on the power of humour.

I truly live in each moment (in as much as I can) but without living as if it were going to be the last moment because I know not when the last moment will arrive and, therefore I should embrace time that has been gifted to me.

I endeavour to give a lot knowing that it cannot always be the best for some, yet I wish them well as they navigate their journey through their own expectation.

I am eternally grateful for the many opportunities that have presented themselves in many guises yet know and acknowledge that luck and coincidence lend a hand.

I will look back upon my many achievements and moments of pride, but I am humbled by those whose grace and integrity never sought the limelight.

I will look back upon all that I have accomplished and will remember those who have helped me to secure those accomplishments.

I will no longer focus my energies on others to the extent that I have but rather give my energies to a more noble cause, one whereby I concentrate on merely pursuing a simple existence and endeavour to live a life of care and compassion.

In a world where the many human values we cherish are often belittled and watered down there is really a lot I cannot influence nor control, yet I can live my life in a way that is about committing to caring, acts of compassion and love and doing, so this can be my message.

These are my conclusions so far and in reaching them I have had many lessons – some straightforward, some a little less so, and some painful.

Ultimately, you have very little control over most things, so it's not worth getting worked up by many of them, and therefore choose only to focus on that which you really have control over.

Ultimately, most of it doesn't really matter, so choose, but choose wisely what you wish to expend your time and energy on.

2. 'Social Technology' – there is a real need for us to learn to interact again ... meaningfully!

The richer we have become, the poorer we become morally and spiritually. We have learned to fly in the air like birds and swim in the sea like fish, but we have not learned the simple art of living together like brothers.
Martin Luther King Jr.

The world is a marvel of technology these days. I am amazed and blown away by the technological advances of the last number of decades. Those growing up these days take them for granted of course and have no idea how far we have *travelled* in recent years, not because they don't care, but when the look at their screens now, be that mobile phone, tablet, laptop, and the like, they can't possibly imagine what came before, or how it was.

Even when the first computer games emerged alongside video, PCs, and CD players, it really was an amazing time to be around, to be part of the generation who tried, tested, and sampled, to be in effect technological guinea pigs in many ways.

I remember having my first CB radio, my first tv-radio-cassette player combo... wow!! The TV was only three inches in size, and it was in black and white but wow. I remember seeing a CD for the first time. I was in Cork, and I was about 11 or 12 maybe, and was surprised how small vinyl had become!

My, how technology has moved, the possibilities are endless. But there's something wrong – don't get me wrong, I'm not criticising technology in the slightest, but my worry is (and has been for a while) that we lose or have lost ourselves somewhat in all of this. For example, when was the last time you wrote a letter? When was the last time you savoured the scratchy sound on vinyl?

Technology is moving at such a pace that I believe we are slowly losing our ability to interact – of course we still meet up for a coffee, go for a drink, visit and so on but the systems and structures that drive society means our ability to interact and connect are slowly being eroded – so much of life now is lived online: paying bills, ordering products, chatting, etc.

And as someone who appreciates what technology can bring to our lives, i.e., keeping in contact with people who live abroad, medical advances, scientific discoveries, entertainment, and leisure, the problem with this is that there are so many more decisions to make, passwords to remember, menus to choose from, boxes to tick, links to click and so on which creates more stress and ultimately erodes our ability to make decisions.

In his book *Team Human*, Douglas Rushkoff argues that 'Human beings rely on the organic world to maintain our prosocial attitudes and behaviours. Online relationships are to real ones like internet pornography is to making love. The artificial experience not only pales in comparison to the organic one, but degrades our understanding of human connection. Our relationships become about metrics, judgements, and power — the likes and follows of a digital economy, not the resonance and cohesions of a social ecology.'[2]

Haim Harari describes how we 'live longer, but we think shorter'[3] whilst Steve Hilton highlights how a lack of freedom to play is causing long-term damage to children describing how they are 'enclosed in school and home, enclosed in cars to shuffle between them, enclosed by fear, by surveillance and poverty and enclosed in rigid schedule of time'.[4]

Pankaj Mishra, argues that the pursuit of likes and followers on social media 'have boosted ordinary image consciousness among millions into obsessive self-projection' whilst 'digital platforms are programmed to map these compulsive attempts at self-presentation (or, self-prettification)'.[5] Jamie Smartt talks about how communication, technology and information is accelerating leading to a 'speedy mind' which in his words is the 'single biggest cause of stress, lack of confidence and bad decisions' leading to 'time poverty, strained relationships, fumbled goals, poor performance and unrealized potential'.[6]

According to one study, a user touches their smartphone 2,167 times daily,[7] whilst the 'Internet has turned out to be an excellent weapon of sabotage [providing]... the tools to verbally and emotionally attack each other'.[8]

Whilst I'm supportive of technology I have a simple approach – I decide when I use it and therefore technology does not decide for me – essentially (and admittedly not always possible but where I can) I stick to text, Facebook and e-mail – that's essentially the three mechanisms I use for communicating with people.

Social media seems to control us these days and thus the need to get a handle on it is more important than ever. Rather than keep developing social media, I recommend we start developing *Social Technology*, that is getting back to engaging and fully interacting with people.

There are of course some people you don't want to interact with and would prefer to avoid. However, the idea of meaningful engagement (and not just interaction) with people should become a priority again especially in an era where so much has been lost to Covid.

With that in mind, here are some thoughts on how we could develop an approach that reduces our use of social media and encourages a greater commitment to Social Technology:

- **Make the effort to 'go back' to pen and paper**: we all of course still use pen and paper for lots of things but technology, e.g., phones, tablets, laptops, etc., have taken over so much that any cafe you go into now, it's almost a novelty to find someone writing. Take time to just to *rediscover* the art of writing – it's almost therapeutic and people do notice, and sometimes they even comment on it.

- **Communicating in person**: we spend so much time looking down now at our screens that we miss valuable opportunities to engage with others – so next time (unless you must) keep your phone in your pocket and start a conversation with someone or just even look around you and observe what's going on.
- **Social Apps**: you most likely have dozens of apps on your phone – why not think of people as apps and so next time you are going to open an app why not use the theme of that app as a conversation starter.
- **Rediscovering Pen-Pal**: does this even exist now? I'm sure it does – contact an old friend, even someone on Facebook from overseas who you are not really in contact with and write them a letter. Yeah, I know it's time consuming and why do that when you can message or mail them. But try it, give it a go, see the effect it has.
- **Turning off your phone or putting it on silent**: even for a short period of time, say half an hour per day and then extend it to say an hour the following week. Allow yourself space and time just to enjoy not being controlled by the phone and rather you take control of it by deciding when you're available.
- **Taking Phone calls**: only take calls from people you know; set your phone up to ensure that people understand they can leave a message or to message you – if it's important, people will leave a message – this way you get to decide when you play the message back if it's important to respond to it.
- **Making Phone calls**: literally just phone up one of your friends and say hi, just a quick hello and don't get into any conversation – literally a 15-second call to say hello, hope all is good, wish them well and off you go again. It will make both of you smile and your friends will be

pleasantly surprised and appreciate it. Even if they don't answer just leave a message.

- **Internet**: if you can do without it (and I'm talking about other than needing it for work), do without it. Go to a cafe where there is no internet – you might even meet interesting people.
- **Twitter**: choose not to have a twitter account or turn it off for a bit – same for Instagram and any other social media accounts.
- **Technology**: start to view it as a tool to be used rather than having any intrinsic meaning in itself.
- **Don't sign up**: for all the packages that offer you this, that and the other. You then feel compelled to watch them because you paid for them. There is plenty of options on mainstream television and if you want to see a new film, just go to the cinema – I know it's more expensive but make it an event occasionally and enjoy the whole experience. Or maybe even get rid of your television and just sit and listen to music or radio or a podcast. I got rid of my TV recently and do not miss it in the slightest.
- **People Watching**: next time you're in a cafe or sitting in a park and similar don't lift your phone – just people watch. It can be interesting at worst and entertaining at best and reflect on your thoughts as they come into your head. Consider why you are thinking what you are thinking when you see different people.
- **Smiling**: give people a smile – it can completely transform a moment with another person.
- **I-Random Acts of Kindness (I-RAK)**: – perform a random act of kindness for someone, even a stranger, just think how you'd feel if someone did something like that for you – you know it creates a very positive feeling.
- **Networking**: go along to a meeting or an event you might not normally be inclined too. You never know who you

might meet or how the conversations might stimulate your thoughts and opinions, or the opportunities that suddenly present themselves when you're least expecting it.

- **Ted Talks**: if you're going to check out internet then check out the Ted Talks – they always provide inspiration and are a good way of helping us to think about our lives and what's important.
- **Walk**: take a little time to go for a walk just to give yourself some space from 'stuff'.
- **Shower**: don't just have a wash, take time to just relax and consider the thoughts that flow through your head – showers are great for helping to clear a busy mind or clarify the many thoughts in your mind.
- **Reduce your social media**: ultimately all you need is one e-mail account, one form of social media and a phone for texting and making and taking phone calls.
- **Leave Notes**: leave notes in random places for strangers to pick but keep the messages only positive.
- **Postcards**: write a postcard to someone from a random place and post it or just address to a friend you don't know and pick a random address.

There are of course many other ways you can try *Social Technology* – you might have even thought of them as you have been reading this. Try it, it can be fun, will certainly be different, and will help you develop or re-ignite your imagination or sense of creativity again.

Social Technology is something we need to get back to again – the world is in need of it more than ever!

3. Learn to know the brain, your brain – what it does, how it works, and most importantly how it fools you

Smart people learn from everything and everyone, average people from their experience, stupid people already have all the answers.
Socrates

If you ever make time to read about how the brain works, it really is truly remarkable. We of course take it for granted, even if unintentionally so, such is its natural endeavour that we don't even think about it. But when you begin to read up on it, and there are, of course, several excellent books on the list (I provide later in the book) that are a good place to start, you really get a sense of the complexity, enormity, and uniqueness of that which is utterly central to our everyday survival, never mind any other bodily function.

A few years ago, I began to buy (and read of course) various books (also on my recommended reading list) that are geared towards demonstrating how we think (as opposed to how we think we think), and the (all too often negative) effect it has on us.

An outcome from this is being more aware of how the brain tricks us and therefore how we should really be thinking instead. From this we can 'train' our mind (as it were) by altering our thinking in ways that will make it easier to navigate life from day to day.

This of course is entirely useful regarding how we behave and apply our attitudes or our being able to shape a response when required. There is no end of these types of books available. Take a walk into any of the main high street bookshops, or you'll notice them (in particular) at airports, many of the *self-help-change-your-life-think-like-the-author-and-you-can-have-a-life-like-*

me variety which offer step by step exercises and daily routines to achieve the new you.

These of course are perfectly fine in their own right, and if they work for you, great. But – and there is a but – it's by no means a criticism of their veracity, however, if you are going to work on coaching yourself and your thinking, you're as well knowing how the machine works before you begin to fine-tune it.

I see no point in reaffirming yourself every day with an activity from a self-help guide if you don't know how and why your brain keeps dishing out negative thoughts in the first place. If you're a brain surgeon and you're reading this, then you might choose to just ignore me. However, if not, my recommendation is not to start with the self-help stuff first but get to know how the brain operates so you know what steps will work for you.

The reality of the brain is that there is so much that we don't know about it. Our brains are not fixed, and they react differently depending on any given situation.

Our natural state is one of daydreaming, our brains are underused, and they are built for and designed to look for patterns even when they don't exist. They have a problem with accepting things that happen randomly.

They mislead, fool, and deceive us continuously (without our even knowing it), they operate at two speeds – the quick thinking and irrational, and the slower, more deliberate, and rational.

The brain frequents Fight, Flight, or Freeze modes regularly, it has a bias for simplicity, is limited to a number of functions (estimated to be six – thought, behaviour, emotions, and memory, as well as basic life functions such as breathing and heart rate) and operates in ways unbeknownst to us most of the time. The good news, however, is that we are not at fault for the brains we have been lumbered with nor the thoughts that come with it.

One of our challenges as humans is to achieve a greater sense of self-awareness, for example, to know when your mind is playing tricks on you, or when you're talking bullshit, or when you have just embellished a story, or perhaps re-created a memory, but in a slightly different way because it fits to a particular conversation you are having in a particular given moment.

In the past when I was recalling from memory a story to someone (or some people) about a previous funny incident, for example, I hadn't perhaps noticed it wasn't as accurate as my previously telling of the story. I am now more conscious of 'the voice' in my own head telling me when it is not quite the same as I had recollected. Unless of course, when I've had a few beers, then it's different voices I hear in my head!

Joking aside, this is perhaps a result of my confusing a story with something closely resembling it (and not a deliberate attempt to distort it), but at least these days I'm much more aware of it, and more importantly can rationalise why I might have confused the two.

There are specific ways in which the brain works that unless we are aware of it, we don't even realise it's happening, and recalling a story from memory is one of those occasions. Try it – next time you're reciting a story to someone about a situation, think about whether you have recalled it as exactly as you did the previous time you told the story.

Two wonderful books I read some years ago that demonstrate vividly how our brain fools us are, Rolf Dobelli's *The Art of Thinking Clearly* and David Mc Rainey's *You Are Not So Smart, Why Your Memory Is Mostly Fiction, Why You Have Too Many Friends on Facebook and 46 Other Ways You Are Deluding Yourself.*

If ever you had any doubt about the way our brains fool us, then you need to read these. If you are convinced of your own ability for working things out or if you are convinced you understand things, even when you know little about a subject, then make time to read these.

One of the key messages from both these books is how our brain has great difficulty in dealing with the idea of randomness – we are always looking for patterns and we have great difficulty in accepting the notion that things just happen, sometimes for no reason, hence why we tend to be often very sceptical or even cynical, or just refusing to believe in certain things, even when there exists lots of evidence. As Charles Seife tells us, 'Our very brains revolt at the idea of randomness. We have evolved as a species to become exquisite pattern finders.'[9]

We are convinced of our ability to work things out or reach conclusions on even the flimsiest of evidence. In fact, we over-estimate our ability completely, and our collective capacity for assessing probability is underwhelming to say the least.

To demonstrate, political science writer Philip Tetlock evaluated more than 28, 000 predictions of nearly 300 political experts over a period of 20 years and famously concluded that 'a dart throwing chimpanzee'[10] would have fared better.

John Brockman contributes that this is in part due to a 'combination of an ever-shortening news cycle, near-instantaneous communications, fragmented markets, heightened competition for viewership and our cognitive and emotional biases' which lessen our capacity to understand what 'large-scale data analyses reveal'.[11]

Awareness of your complicity in indulging your own fantasies about how much you understand a subject or subjects is equal to also understanding the kind of mindset you possess.

Being acutely aware of how your values and beliefs inform your outlook, i.e., the opinions, ideas, questions, and thoughts you might have, and where these come from is more than beneficial.

As someone who describes himself these days as being secular-humanist, I'm acutely aware of the thoughts that gather in my own mind when, for example, I hear the views of Evangelicals on TV or radio or the internet or when I engage directly in conversation with Christians.

Whilst I might disagree fundamentally with them or anyone from any religion on a particular issue, I also observe and uphold the ideas of freedom of speech and individuals having entitlement to their opinion, such is my conviction in this regard.

Of course, given the strength of belief I hold against any sentiment, words or deed that might contravene basic human rights, for example, discrimination against someone because of the colour of their skin, or their ability, or their sexual preference, I'm acutely aware of my frame of mind when an Evangelist might articulate something like, 'it's against God's law for two men to love one another'.

At one level I couldn't give a hoot if two men shack up with one another if it's consensual, but at an emotional level, I do care fundamentally that the basic right to love whom you choose to love is upheld, irrespective of anyone else's view or declaration.

The importance of knowing not only how the brain itself works is vitally important, but to know how your own mind works, is without sounding like stating the blindingly obvious, a must. Although, over the last number of years, I have engaged with many who seem more interested in simply being right about things than truly learning about how they interpret, perceive and understand things.

The problem is that until we make time to consider how our own mind works, be it how we reach the conclusions we do, or perhaps articulate the beliefs we have, or even offer our *tuppence-worth* when called upon, most of us will not really understand how our brain works.

To give you a sense of this, how many times have you suddenly offered an opinion on a subject you know little about but when it came up in conversation you suddenly sounded like an expert (or at least to yourself you did) – where did that come from exactly?

It stands to reason that if you know how you think and why you think what you think or where your thoughts might come from then you're better able to cope, better able to deal with *shit*, better able to control your responses and reactions, and perhaps, ultimately the outcomes from a particular situation.

To be aware of, and know your own *triggers* and *stressors*, or how you perceive the words or actions of others and how to change the complexion of any situation is vital. Perhaps knowing that we are *hardwired* in particular ways, or that we inevitably categorise things to ease our understanding, or we fill in missing information we're not even aware of is one of the many blind spots we possess.

We have evolved from an environment when things were scarce over not only centuries but millennia so we were able to keep ourselves in check (so to speak) but now we can massage our ego and exercise our desires without needing to think about our actions or even account for its impact on the environment or ecological systems, or the outcomes it has for others, e.g., buying cheap clothing on the high street without considering whether it has been produced in *sweat shops* somewhere in Asia.

We have evolved to not only desire status but to actively pursue it alongside social standing among our colleagues, friends, family, neighbours and the wider community and view this as a sense of reward or entitlement for our efforts. We struggle to detach ourselves from people who affect our emotions yet (equally), we only feel a sense of assurance when we believe we know or think we know exactly how those same people feel about us.

As we have evolved over time, so too has the size and capacity of our brains, but whereas in the past survival was our priority in addition to being able to function co-operatively within small groups of people, our capacity to think has also evolved and that has brought with it its own challenges, e.g., motivation, perception, decision-making, etc.

Knowing how the brain works is one thing, knowing how your mind works is another thing, knowing how your brain fools you is an entirely good thing!

4. Work out what annoys you ... and then work out how to deal with it

Be careful to leave your sons well instructed rather than rich, for the hopes of the instructed are better, than the wealth of the ignorant.
Epictetus

We humans are a funny bunch, funny in the sense of our traits and habits, and not necessarily our humour, although to be fair there are plenty who fall into that category for sure. How we apply ourselves in particular situations, how we shoot ourselves in the foot, bite our noses to spite our face, and all those other well-worn over-used clichés do reflect something inherently contradictory about our nature, or as some would argue, our natures.

How we use, for example, information to suit ourselves, how we lie to avoid arguments with our nearest and dearest, how we make up bullshit and express opinions about topics we know nothing about and/or opinions we never knew we had an opinion on until a conversation about the same was had. Yes, that's the kind of funny I'm really talking about!

Politicians use statistics to tell us a story dug out of a report, perhaps one *good* statistic only, when the rest was nonsense, or they remind us that we've had two-quarters growth as if we should not only understand what the significance of it is but that we should feel the impact of it.

Investors set up businesses in already squeezed urban settings where employees end up having to move into and be *forced* to live in cramped, over-priced accommodation with strangers, and breathe in the same over-polluted air generated by too many businesses operating at the same time.

Alternatively, you can immerse yourself in long commutes each day and in doing so turn a third of your day into half a day that is work related. It just doesn't make sense in real terms does it, but it very much becomes part of our everyday lives, and more worryingly, such arrangements become very normalised.

Humans cheat because we are unsure whether the other person will behave as we would like them too, so we cheat anyway on the presumption that they will. We want to resolve conflicts, but we don't talk to the people we need to resolve our conflict with but if we do, we find it so difficult to listen to their story, so we prepare our answers in advance.

We wait until we or someone close to us has a near death experience (or dies) before we reflect on our lives and assess what is important. We tend to make decisions based on outcomes that suit us but rarely consider the true impact of that decision or decisions on other people.

We measure our self-worth based on material items and often procrastinate so we don't have to leave ourselves open to scrutiny. Leaving ourselves open to scrutiny is one of those things that is uncomfortable because we are left feeling not only vulnerable but exposed with the risk of being humiliated and yet when we reflect on these moments, we most probably could have better anticipated it.

We become annoyed in these moments, in part because not only were we not ready but we then have to confront why we are annoyed, and of course, we sometimes choose denial as opposed to honesty, because honesty of course, is to take responsibility and assume control of our lives. If we do, we get to know ourselves on a much more intimate level.

One of the problems with not knowing the things that annoy you or get under your skin is that they tend to creep up on you without warning. For example, it might be a situation when someone does or says something, or during a discussion that you suddenly realise you have an opinion on a subject or matter that you didn't know you had.

Sometimes you carry around a feeling where something is gnawing at you, or you find yourself in poor form for no apparent reason and can't quite work out what is bothering you. It can be a conversation you had with someone earlier in the day, a piece of news you received from someone the day before, or an issue that is on the horizon but you're not truly aware how much it is affecting you until it's upon you. The secret therefore is recognising when it is happening and acknowledging it, particularly before it does.

I've always had what I can describe as 'a temper'; of course everyone has a temper, or to be more precise, temperament. In my case, I was prone to getting angry or having a 'short fuse' and I had to learn to master it over the years. I could never quite work out what it was that set me off in my younger years – I just knew I had to learn to control it. I have largely mastered it although from time to time it does flare up although these days what tends to set me off is my laptop doing random things without warning (which was much more common with my old laptop) and my bouts of wanting to bounce it off the table or drop kick it into touch have radically reduced.

I am of course older now, and arguably wiser, and my escape clause is a mantra I use to good effect, i.e., *it is what it is*, which I find allows me, in true Scooby-Doo style, to cut my temper off at the pass. Of course, whilst having mantras or mottos to live by is useful, they are limited, if, for example, someone is trying to deliberately antagonise you. If someone is in your face 'giving it lilty' (as we say in these parts), it's not so easy just to say 'he's a dick', and 'it is what it is' and simply walk away. This I get but how we react is still ultimately a choice, our choice, and therefore to minimise the risks we need to recognise the things that we react to.

The best way to do this is to simply make time for yourself, away from distractions, in a quiet space, and just take time to think about things. And ask yourself the following question – what exactly bothers me? And with pen and paper by your side, start to jot down the things that bother you. And be honest with yourself – allow yourself to put them down on paper.

There are things that often annoy us but for different reasons we go into denial and don't acknowledge them. By recognising what bothers us allows us to release ourselves from the guilt or shame that is often attached to feeling this way, and we can begin the process of working out how we deal with them.

You can't of course stop the feelings that come with certain things but what you can do is recognise that they exist and then begin to learn how to manage them. And once it becomes clearer, you are in a better position to respond accordingly, accepting them as part of you, your nature, and being okay with it. Recognition is always the first step, followed by acceptance and then learning how to manage your response. So, take time, take the first step, work out what annoys you.

5. Rarely is anything as it appears

Diamonds are not very beautiful in the raw state. It is the skill of the Diamond Cutter that reveals the beauty of the diamond.
Edward De Bono

In years gone by, it all seemed so simple. Textbooks on a variety of subjects provided you with a particular narrative. Any textbook could be wrong of course, and new books published might critique said textbooks to demonstrate why they were wrong. As we evolved and learned new things, new conclusions were reached and so we continued to progress. As more books were published revealing new information, new truths came to light.

Since then, the internet was birthed, and whilst its creator had a very different idea of what it was set up to do – very far from how it is being used in the modern era, the advent of social media has most certainly challenged conventional thinking as to how we learn.

Social media has created a wealth of experts in every subject imaginable. Covid, for example, has proven that a gym instructor in Ireland can develop an expertise in virology overnight, whilst a labourer on a building site in England suddenly reveals his epidemiologist credentials.

People create memes which compare information or images with a 'plot line' plastered over them to make a point, and then people share them, and like a wildfire they are re-shared again and again, and before you know it, everyone is an expert! Well, this is just one way people assert their previously undeclared knowledge.

If there's one thing that Covid or the BLM protests have taught me in 2019, 2020 and 2021 is that some of my colleagues, even friends and family, and many others for whom I had credited with as possessing relatively good critical thinking skills, have left me somewhat surprised.

It wasn't or isn't so much the opinions they possessed but when you flag up the irony, hypocrisy or contradictory nature of their posts, or where there are holes in their arguments, very few would reflect upon it as an opportunity to learn from but choose to dig their heels in and defend their beliefs, almost as if they were welded to them, and under no account would they consider reviewing them.

If there is anything that experience has taught me, it is that rarely are things as they appear. And I don't mean that when you stand in front of a blue car, it isn't blue. I'm talking more about things that are open to interpretation, e.g., opinions are expressed about a set of circumstances, where the actions of someone or others is defined in a particular way and so on.

Let me offer you an example. In 2020, I took in a lodger for a period. She was originally from Ukraine but had been living in the UK and Ireland for quite some time. Among the languages she spoke was Russian. This is an important detail as will become apparent. One evening, she got very drunk, and her behaviour ended up being completely unacceptable, so much so that I threatened to phone the police on her.

I won't go into detail but let's just say it was like having a teenager at home again on one of those bad teenage nights. I threatened to phone the police on her as a last resort thinking it might trigger in her a response that might encourage her to 'cop on'.

Next thing I know, she's on the phone to her father, who used to be a Russian Diplomat, and he wanted to speak to me about what was happening. I refused such was my desire not to be drawn further into an unnecessary discussion.

When she finally went off to her bed and peace ensued, I had to speak to her the next day, and of course, she didn't have much memory of the whole episode. Anyway, somewhat embarrassed by the situation, she went off to spend some time at her cousin's place for a couple of weeks (to my great relief).

Not long after that, in fact within a week, a package arrived at my door from Amazon. I rarely order anything online and so it came as a bit of surprise, but even more surprisingly it was addressed to me. It had no delivery note, and no return address, and so I had no idea where it came from, but inside was a brand-new Samsung phone.

Now, if you are like me, you believe that random packages just don't arrive at your door without a reason. I thought my kids got together to buy me a phone but when I checked, they all said no. I checked with my lodger if she had ordered something, and she said no – I thought maybe she felt guilty and wanted to make some reparation for her behaviour.

So here I was with this brand-new phone with absolutely no idea where it came from. What was interesting was that it had come from overseas as it contained a two-pin charger. None of this made any sense!

Okay, so I was unable to trace who – not my kids, nor my lodger, so I put it on charge in any case thinking okay, I can't return it, I have no idea where it has come from and so I might as well use it. I then turned it on and the language that greeted me was Russian – yes, Russian!

And thus, the only conclusion I could reach was that my lodger's father, embarrassed by the situation that arose involving his daughter, decided to make reparation on her behalf. Of course, she had denied that she or anyone connected to her had sent any package.

For months I was convinced that her father had sent the package, but everyone was in denial. I had no delivery note, I couldn't return it, and as my own phone was old and failing, I thought okay, what to do, just keep and use it. Occasionally the story of the mystery phone would come up in conversation, and I would simply tell everyone, that my lodger's father had sent it out of some form of guilt – a random phone turns up at my door after the whole episode and the language is in Russian – there can of course be no other rational explanation.

Fast forward and in November 2021, I travelled with my son to Budapest for a few days to catch up with some friends, some of whom joined us from Germany. In all the catch-up stories we shared, I explained to them the whole story of this mystery phone and how my lodger's father had sent it. Both my friends found the story funny, but more so my friend and colleague Dominik, whom I have known for about 15 years and have worked with a lot over the years.

After I had finished my story, he was still laughing. I thought that he really enjoyed the story, that my storytelling skills were as sharp as ever! There was more to it than that. He showed me a picture on his phone, or rather an image of a receipt for a phone he had recently ordered. At first, I wasn't quite sure what it related to but then I saw the type of phone – a Samsung A20e – well that's the same phone as mine... and then it dawned on me. *What? You ordered it? Really? Like, for real?*

He just sat there and laughed, hence why he found my whole story funny – not my telling the story! He was listening to me describing things in intimate detail and (in particular), my attempt at trying to work out how this phone came to be at my place. The mystery had been solved. Dominik had very kindly ordered me a phone – asked why, he told me he had grown annoyed listening to my complaining how my phone (at the time) was always running into probs, and how I was having to use a variety of phones for different reasons, and because I was struggling financially at the time, I wasn't able to afford a new phone.

He wasn't annoyed in the sense of him being truly annoyed, but he just decided to put me out of my misery, or rather my old phone, and order me a new one. He had no idea of the episode with my lodger, nor that she spoke Russian, or that her father was Russian, or that the language on the phone was set in Russian. He was completely unaware of all of this, and I don't even think he knew there was no delivery note, so he might have at one point been curious if it was even delivered, or perhaps why I hadn't even mentioned it.

The moral of this story, though, is that it's very easy to draw conclusions based on assumptions, but trust me, as someone who has plenty of experience of doing it quite a bit down the years, more so in my younger years, I have grown to realise that we often interpret things in response to what we know to be true – true to ourselves of course, without knowing what the actual truth is. You see, we assume things, we make judgements, we have no option but to do so because this is how we make sense of the world.

The danger, though, and further to this the challenge we all face, is to know when we are making assumptions, and understand how it can adversely affect our ability to make informed judgements, is being in possession of as much information as we possibly can.

One way of gaining a greater understanding of why things are not always the way they are is to appreciate the concept of 'duality'. In its most simplistic terms, Duality means that a question, for example, can have two very different answers that are equally legitimate.

Often, we see things in simple black and white terms and can't fathom the notion that a question can have two equally opposing answers. Journalists use this a lot in interviews, particularly with politicians, when they pose a question, and expect the politician to answer it one way or the other, without acknowledging that not all answers are in black or white.

It's not always as simple as that because often answers can be complex and nuanced and it's often used as a tactic to get individuals to commit to a position so that it can be used to demonstrate contradiction or hypocrisy. Now, of course, there are some questions that have straightforward answers, but Western culture is alive with the narrative that things must be one way or the other.

I find it not so difficult to hold two opposing views or recognise that two diverse opinions can be equally valid – having raised three children was often a bit of a balancing act between the competing interests of my children and the legitimacy I would bestow upon their musings when they were at loggerheads with one another. Their concerns were legitimate, their opinions valid and even though often diametrically opposed to one another, they could all be right, or all be wrong for that matter. The only time duality didn't apply in this regard was when all three were at odds with one another at the same time. Usually, it would only be two arguing with one another at a given moment and therefore duality was often in play.

Duality in Eastern culture is not so uncommon – the idea that two answers can be equally applicable is far from unheard of, in fact, looking beyond a single answer to any question is positively encouraged. As Jesse J. Prinz describes, people 'are prone to think dialectically, recognizing that two opposing sides may both have some truth to them. This principle is expressed in the idea of Yin and Yang, which are conceptualized as opposing forces existing harmoniously in the universe'.[12]

Susan Cain explains that, 'Westerners value boldness and verbal skill, traits that promote individuality, while Asians prize quiet, humility and sensitivity which foster group cohesion… [No one] is superior to the other but that a profound difference in cultural values has a powerful impact on the personality styles avowed by each culture.'[13]

The Western mindset – without trying to label all Westerners as homogeneous – most certainly seems less able to contemplate the idea of duality but if we are to become better equipped at seeing things beyond their immediate appearance, or to hear and understand much better the words that people utter, we need to bring ourselves around to the idea that duality is not just an idea that exists in physics.

This is of course a process of intentional learning, and it could begin in schools, where we teach children that not every question has one answer. It has to be a deliberate process because as PZ Meyers reminds us, we are 'the result of a chance shuffle of genetic attributes during meiosis, a few number of mutations, and the luck of the draw in the grand sperm race of fertilisation'[14] and so when you started out it was unclear what you would become.

To become more than we are, at least in a physical capacity, the process of learning concepts such as duality must be deliberate because if we want to know what's really going on we need to dig much deeper than we do now because... rarely is anything as it appears!

6. Most ideas are not fixed and are open to scrutiny and subject to review

Science is not truth. Science is finding truth. When science changes its opinion, it didn't lie to you. It learned more.
Unknown

We are taught in life to be consistent, even if there are no actual lessons in consistency at school or college, or even if no one tells you (literally) that you should be consistent. But it's there all the time – we look for consistency in others, in ourselves and so on. I kind of hinted at this in the last lesson, in that those of us in the West have problems with Duality and therefore the idea of any question that has more than one answer, has the potential to appear to be contradictory.

'You've changed' is an oft-proclaimed attack on our character to suggest that we're not consistent and therefore by implication can't be relied upon to meet expectations. Even with our own expectations there is an unwritten rule that we need to be consistent, at least in the eyes of others, and that we should not deviate from our chosen course.

To do anything other than what people might expect of us, or what we even expect of ourselves, is to break some form of custom and practice, because if people are consistent, you can trust them, and trust is essential, right?

We are taught, or brought up to believe even, at least predominantly in Western culture that things can only be black or white, and you have to be one or the other, that there is no grey and you have to make a decision, so much so, that if you don't have a position, you are almost worse than those that take the opposite position on a particular question or subject. At least with those with whom you disagree, you know where you stand with them but if you are neither in agreement or disagreement, you don't know what you're getting and therefore, you cannot be trusted.

I have news for you... life just isn't like that. The reality is that we humans evolve, and we change, and what believe at 17, 24, 40 and older changes. Now, I should point out that these are random ages, so if you're about to turn any of these don't expect a sudden moment of clarification the morning you wake up a year older. We are, however, often led to believe that change is bad, and that if you change, you can't be trusted, or that you will let people down.

The result is that we tend to remain 'stuck', and hold on to certain beliefs or values (even if we're not sure why), and all too often we find out that those individuals that might have been the most critical of us, end up being the one's that change the quickest or change the most significantly. There are moments when we have stuck with something so as to please others only to find out they have changed their position and we are left with the proverbial egg on our face.

So here it is in its simplest form – you can change, and you are allowed to change your views! You are allowed to evolve, you are allowed to learn, you are allowed to reflect upon the views and ideas you hold, even those that are most dear to you. No matter what anyone says, there is no official rule (other than convention, tradition, custom or similar) that says you must stick to a particular idea or opinion for any length of time.

Don't let anyone tell you any different. Now, I'm not talking about flipping ideas and opinion so often that people have no idea where they stand with you, but rather that you can alter or change your ideas and opinion when you learn new things, and that you don't have to stick with them just because you feel obliged to do so. Even if you advocated on behalf of certain ideas or strongly articulated a certain opinion, you can change and here's something novel, you are allowed to change. For example, if you are a parent but acted like the 'archetypal teenager', e.g., drank, smoked, tried drugs, had sex, etc., and suddenly you find that your kids are reaching 'that age' or are already 'dabbling' in teenage behaviour, this is not a cue for you to say, 'well I can hardly stop them from indulging in such behaviour since I was up to it myself', right? WRONG!

The very reason that you did indulge, and you know some of the risks and dangers gives you extra reason to minimise risks. Giving them a green light because you did it out of some form of guilt, does not excuse your responsibilities as a parent. Where your approach can differ is that when you find out what they 'have been up to', you don't react (like perhaps your parents did?) but rather chat with them about it. The message is simple, though, you can change – you don't have to be stuck in a particular position.

I have made mistakes in my past when I stuck to a certain position, or held a certain view, only to find out that those that held me to account the most over my views or opinions ended up being not only the most inconsistent but also the quickest to change their position.

I recall many years ago, on a night out with some friends, during my student days at University of Ulster in Jordanstown, just outside Belfast, there was one particular night that stood out for me that taught me a very clear lesson. We were out in Belfast and had gone for a bite to eat, and some post-bar drinks at a friend's flat and then were trying to find a taxi home. It was proving challenging, and then suddenly, a police Land Rover pulled up. Not your typical kind – if you're not from Northern Ireland, you might need to search police Land Rover, Northern Ireland, early '90s. They were armoured jeeps, designed to absorb gun shots and rocket attacks.

Anyways, I thought, this could be interesting – it was 1993, and things were quite tense in Belfast. And I had assumed somewhat that the police will be suspicious of why five of us are wandering around late at night in this particular area of Belfast.

As it turns out, they were just concerned for our welfare, and wanted to drop us home.

My first reaction was, there is no way am I getting into the back of a Land Rover (at least not late at night in Belfast). I was deeply suspicious. One of the guys with us was quite Republican and very anti-police – guess who was the first into the jeep? Yip, you guessed it. In fact, I wasn't Republican in the slightest and the least anti-police out of all of us, but who was the last person standing trying to convince the rest to get a taxi? Me of course!

Even if the police were concerned and their intentions honourable, someone might take a pot shot at them – we might be the headlines the following day as three police officers and five young students were making their way to a mortuary. I was also a parent at the time and was married back then and so, had to consider my family.

In the end up, I was left with the reality of contemplating the risks associated with wandering around Belfast late at night in an area I was somewhat unfamiliar with, and with a first name like mine (in Northern Ireland, we are often defined by our names), it might evoke certain kinds of response in some sections of the local population that might give me the impression I might not be welcome – injury, torture and death among the alternatives!

I got into the jeep, very reluctantly, trying hard to reconcile my suspicion of the police and my concerns that someone might want to take us out (and I'm not talking for a meal) with that of my being left isolated on my own in the early hours of the morning in Belfast and what might result. Only days later, Belfast was to grab global headlines with the *Shankill Bombing* and only a week later, the *Greysteel Massacre* – these were the times we were living in.

All was good in the end up. The police did indeed leave us home safe, and I was thankful, not least of all for saving us money on a taxi! What was my lesson from the evening? The guy who was the most pro-Republican and anti-police changed his mind in a heartbeat – fear drove him to change his mind to be honest, but all that bragging and tough-talking and propagandising about his Republican credentials went out the window.

I realised that those who shout loudest can very easily throw all their values and principles out the window when the prize is bigger – it doesn't matter the reasons in all honesty, it was just a demonstration that very quickly, those who shout about things the most and the loudest, are often the least principled, or are the quickest to abandon their core beliefs, or to appear to be the most contradictory. Beware these people!

Always remember that anyone unhappy with you changing your mind, that is their problem, it is their reaction, their responsibility. It is not your role or your duty or your obligation to keep them happy at the expense of you having the right to express yourself truly or to be true to what you stand for or believe in.

The Earth is undergoing change every moment of the day – nothing remains the same – humans evolve, it's that simple. Things change because we learn, and the more we learn the greater our capacity for comprehending new ideas grows.

Changing your mind requires of you a particular kind of mindset, one that at first has you believing that you can, secondly you are comfortable with the decisions you make, thirdly that you also feel okay with it, and lastly, you can 'handle' the inevitable flak that will come from some quarters about you changing your mind.

None of us is born with a mindset, it is of course something that evolves over time and is arguably influenced largely by environmental factors, be that our family, where we grow up, what we learn at school, the political system that governs us and so on. There has been plenty of argument going back decades as to whether we humans are already pre-determined (by nature) and thus born to think and behave in a certain way, or perhaps, how we are nurtured over our lifetime, is indeed the ultimate determinant.

Whilst many might argue either way, there is a general acceptance that both your genes and your environment are equally important; for example, there might be those with a propensity for violence in their DNA but depending on the environment where they grow up, that propensity becomes less or greater.

There might be those that are more inclined to demonstrate levels of stress, but if we grow up in a loving family that offers us assurance and not only nurtures in us a sense of calm but teaches how to deal with challenges, those inherent levels of stress might not see the light of day, or at least they are reduced.

A mindset is something that does evolve of course over time and tends to reflect the sum of our experiences enjoyed (or not enjoyed as the case may be) by someone and in turn, informs how they respond to others, how they approach various situations, or how they deal with stress and so on.

It's also true that individuals might be born with the capacity for empathy and grow to act accordingly and so feel compassion towards others in times of anxiety or crisis; or someone without any capacity for empathy who has committed an assault might feel no remorse at all. They might understand a crime has been committed but cannot comprehend the hurt caused to that person.

It's all too easy to merely dismiss people as uncaring, mad, thoughtless, selfish or 'crackpots', but we have got to get to know the mindset of someone who, for example, supports Trump – why would white middle-aged working-class Christian Americans vote for Trump when he is anything but working class and is not remotely religious? Why, at a time when we need reason and intellectualism (and I'm not talking the academic snobbery type that you might find in an exclusive educational institution) more than ever, people seem to be turning away from the very thing that brought us enlightenment?

Why are people seemingly less resilient these days and respond to triggers and stressors more rapidly, especially in an era when we have more capacity to truly assess danger or check reality? Why do parents compete with one another whey they know it makes no sense in real terms and only leads to stress and anxiety and sometimes even worse?

Why are those in power viewed as bad and those who are not, as good? Why do many people view political correctness as a bad thing? Why do we continue to pursue naming and/ or shaming as a deterrent when we know that it is ineffective and fails to change behaviour? Why do we believe personality is fixed, and underestimate the importance of context?

Knowing the mindset of others is of paramount importance in our efforts to get through our lives. It helps us, I believe, to become more patient or at the very least, more tolerant. It helps us tailor our expectations to a level of reality that we can live with and control. It helps us to respond more effectively to what life throws at us and helps us to nurture and generate empathy and compassion for (and in) others and enables us to be less judgemental and live a more stress-free life.

Having a mindset that enables us to do all of this requires quite some capacity. It is of course much easier not to contemplate any of these questions and remain in positions that are more comfortable for us, rather than always be open to the idea of reviewing our ideas, our beliefs, and our values.

Ideas are not fixed, so the next time someone criticises you for changing just say, yes, I'm a human being, I change, we change, we grow, we learn, we evolve and with it our opinions.

My experience is that those who criticise you will do so because they haven't got it in them to evolve, or they will catch you out – they will baffle you by changing after being the most vocal about why you shouldn't change. So don't wait – be the owner of your own thoughts and change when you want or when you feel or think it is time to change.

7. Very little in life is certain

Certainty is the death of wisdom, thought, creativity.
Shekhar Kapur

Someone once said the only thing that's certain is death and taxes (Ben Franklin I believe), unless of course you are a billionaire in which case you might rule out taxes. I jest of course, well mostly – this still is largely true, billionaires, it seems, don't pay much tax but before they reached that status, they did pay some, unless of course they're born into such wealth.

I don't think there is any more that you could add to this exclusive list of two that you couldn't argue against. The one alternative that does spring to mind is that people will surprise you – people will always surprise you, particularly when you least expect it – even those closest to you.

If death is guaranteed, then of course people are born (stating the obvious I know) and of course they must inevitably be having sex. Of course, there is artificial insemination but by and large people come about from what they do naturally – procreate. If death, taxes, and surprises are the guarantees in life, then the assumption is that nothing else is guaranteed.

Most of us grow up in a world where much of our experience already has a degree of certainty about it – going to school, maybe onto further education, job, marriage, and children, although in recent times that pattern is changing. In most cultures, and of course, most countries this tends to be the path set out for us and whilst this varies from country to country, region to region and culture to culture, it's safe to assert that that is how it has been for some time.

The reality in the modern era is that many of those traditions that we have perhaps taken for granted or assumed were 'the norm' are no longer guaranteed. Jobs are no longer readily available – automation (among other things) is seeing to that, the family unit is changing beyond the traditional notion of husband, wife and children, divorce rates are increasing and access to education is not as accessible as it once was – costs and availability among other obstacles.

The world almost feels that it is in constant turmoil or transition, be that conflict in various corners of the planet, the vast acceleration in technology or climate change. These alone bring with them much stress, anxiety, depression, pressure, and indecision. Not least of all, contributing to this is how we now consume more information in an hour than we once did in an entire week, or even a month, and for previous generations, arguably a year, perhaps even a lifetime.

Our ability to make decisions, and informed decisions (at that) are proving more difficult than at any point in history. We often feel overwhelmed, and this is in part because most of us are always switched on. 'Communication, technology and information: they're accelerating, getting more pervasive and more compelling, with no signs they will ever slow down,'[15] Jamie Smartt writes.

All that seemed so familiar is no longer so, yet we are still preparing people for *the journey* – do well at school and you can go onto university, graduate from university and you'll get a job. Get a job, you'll be successful and happy and then you meet someone, and you settle down and start a family and live happily ever after. No one prepares you for what might be the reality of not making it through school, or even if you do but maybe not make it on to university, or if you do you leave with lots of debt and might not get the job you want and end up working a variety of jobs post-graduation just to survive. The aspirations and dreams that were nurtured in you by parents, teachers, lecturers or otherwise, might not materialise.

The certainties that once were, are no longer certainties and so we need to prep ourselves for all sorts of eventualities and that means the need to adapt, to tailor our expectations, to be pragmatic, realistic, and resilient are necessary.

In addition to working towards certain goals and aspirations, we also need to know the reality of the world we live in. For example, by reaffirming that everyone can follow their dreams or that you can be anything you want to be, we need to qualify these statements and explain the difficulties and challenges faced.

Yes, of course you can excel, you can exceed expectations, you can fulfil goals, but not everybody will, and most won't, not because of a lack of desire, of course, but other factors are at play – luck, opportunity, right time, right place, right people, etc.

Things have changed in recent times – the advance in technology means we live much if not most of our lives through our phones now, or rather, almost all that we need can be brought to us through our phones. Alongside the development in mobile technology, we have social media, 24-hour television including countless channels and reality TV no less. YouTube has unleashed a whole generation of 'influencers' alongside other mediums such as Instagram and TikTok.

You can become a celebrity almost overnight. You don't need to audition anymore, you don't need to sign up to record labels, you can create your own videos and so on. Instant gratification is *the currency* and because you can reach a global audience almost instantly you don't need to pursue traditional methods. All of this has brought enhanced expectations about what can be achieved.

Paul Gilbert writes that, 'It's very easy for us to absorb values from the media, attitudes that are pervading our working lives, and not appreciate their negative effects on our minds and relationships. So, we can end up with overestimated incentive systems in our personal goal seeking and lose focus on many other facets of our lives.'[16]

George Monbiot alludes to research psychologists in the US having carried out where 'among pre-teens and young teenagers, the degree to which their values were pro-social or anti-social: the more they engaged in social media, the less socially oriented their values became'.[17]

This has created a generation who believe that not only can they achieve and have the means to do so at their disposal, but often exhibit a sense of entitlement regarding this. They have in many ways come to expect as opposed to hope for, but the reality is that very little is certain, and we need to nurture an understanding of this in people, and furthermore the ability to deal with the reality that this brings, inevitably disappointment, and how individuals need to be able to manage the emotions that this brings.

8. Very few people really appreciate the value of money – we need to know and understand the true value of money

Money doesn't make you happy. I now have $50 million. I was just as happy when I had $48 million.
Arnold Schwarzenegger

The value of money is completely relative. The price of a super-duper-wuper frappa-wappachino in New York might feed a family of four for a day in a refugee camp in Jordan. Where I live a neighbour of mine recently sold his house for £165, 000 – a 5-bedroom and two-living room detached property in a nice rural area.

The same house in London or Dublin would probably go for at the very least, three-quarters of a million pounds, if not arguably more, depending on the area. I can buy a bottle of Coke in a shop where I live for around £1.60 but almost without fail in any airport it will cost the equivalent of €3 (approx. £2.80) or more.

My point is not about the reasons as to why there is a difference and the reasons for this but rather that we don't really understand the value of money. How can a good quality house where I live in Northern Ireland, which is surrounded by countryside, the air is cleaner, the environment healthier, there's less traffic and I'm 25 minutes' drive from beaches in both directions be worth between 5–6 times less than a house in London? It's not logical and doesn't make much sense – it can't simply be about the law of supply and demand.

I get it in many ways – London is a great city, has a great vibe, it's attractive, a lot happens there but as we often discover, many people look to get out of a city like London in the end. They want to move away, get closer to nature, have cleaner air, more green space and, of course, be paying much less for their property, be that buying or renting. Just getting out of London can take quite some time, be that by car or public transport so none of it stands to reason why a property with much less of everything might cost six to seven times more.

Some years back, a colleague of mine was over from London at an event I had organised and as her flight wasn't until the evening, I offered to show her around the area. I had to drop some things off at home first and as we parked in front of my house, she noticed a 'For Rent' sign in the house next door.

She was surprised at the asking price per month – something like £420 per month – 'Is that for one room?' she asked curiously. Just as she was surprised at the rental fee, I was surprised at her question. 'No that's for the house,' I responded. I explained it was a three-bedroomed semi-detached which had a back garden also. In London she was paying almost three times as much – for a one-bedroom apartment – albeit she was living in or around Chelsea so that bumps the price up no end.

Such is the normalisation of these things, i.e., by just saying she lives in Chelsea (if you happen to know the reputation of the area) gives it credibility – the question of why someone would pay almost three times as much for renting a small apartment in a building with many others as opposed to having a three-bedroomed house doesn't even come into it.

We just shrug our shoulders, accept it, and acknowledge that living in any big city comes with a price, but still it doesn't make much sense, in fact it just doesn't stand to reason, yet we accept it and normalise it with a shrug and justification that is oft offered to us when we ask the same question.

It can't always have been like this, right? When did it change? And when did it become normal that someone becomes okay with what is in effect a bit of lunacy. Perhaps it becomes normalised when we don't even ask the question why it has become normalised.

In 2019, I worked in Dublin for about 6 months and my monthly rent for an ensuite room in a five-bedroomed house (without a living room) that I shared with seven others was at least four times more expensive than the mortgage on my own three-bedroomed house. Again, the law of supply and demand I suppose, but of course it can't be as simple as just that. There are lots of reasons as to how it gets to that point, and this happens over years rather than waking up one day and it's like this.

We've become so accustomed to things being like this that we don't stop to really reflect upon what our money gets us. We have ideas about what things cost or should cost relative to our normal circumstances or the situation we find ourselves in. We take out a mortgage and we don't stop to think what that might buy us in other countries.

If the cost of a Happy Meal for two children in the West equates to that of buying a basic shelter for a refugee family which might last for no less than a couple of weeks, then how can this be? The needs of the refugee family are much greater than a very average bite-to-eat that will be quickly forgotten about. And more importantly, why don't we really stop to think about that?

Consider how much we spend at key times of the year – Xmas, Birthdays, anniversaries etc. For example, why can't we have something like an airline that offers fixed-price flights – yes of course, there are days of the week when it's more popular to fly, or when people want to get away, but why can't we just have an airline that charges the same price no matter what journey you make – wouldn't that be such a novelty? Or a hotel that charges you the same price no matter when you book. Airlines and hotels, among many industries, could still offer all sorts of deals; like what difference does it make to an airline when you fly or a hotel when you book, so long as the rooms or seats are booked.

A plane when it is filled with fuel doesn't know the difference between a Tuesday and Saturday, the same goes for a hotel room. Of course, they are not sentient beings so it might sound like stating the obvious, and we know it's about generating profits, but maybe just maybe, it could be something that could be tried – the 'no matter when' deal. Wouldn't that be nice? Wouldn't that help us get a better understanding of value, i.e., the cost of something is based on a particular formula, rather than supply and demand?

Very few of us really appreciate the value of money – we need to appreciate this more and understand its true value. Perhaps the growing discontent among Earth's population with the various systems of governance we are subject to, perhaps that discontent can bring about a change in attitude towards money.

9. Most people can't and won't be entrepreneurs and innovators

Work for a cause, not for applause. Live life to express not to impress. Don't strive to make your presence noticed, just make your absence felt. Feel the legacy, not just the money.
Unknown

As technology has evolved at an alarmingly lightning speed in recent years, and with it the automation that has resulted, many of our traditional industries have disappeared or shifted continent; jobs we once did (and took somewhat for granted) have been replaced, or in many cases, no longer exist.

In fact, there was a time when (whilst not always guaranteed) work existed on a regular and consistent basis. Even if you left school without qualifications, there was a good chance, that with effort and a bit of luck, you'd end up with work of some kind, maybe not quite what you were looking for, but consistent paid work, nonetheless.

These days, there are no guarantees – we live in an era of what's become known as the 'gig economy' and in order to survive, you might have to reinvent yourself several times over throughout the duration of your career, and go from starting out in the career you love to bouncing from one industry to another, or ensuring you have capacity for 'transferability' where you can apply yourself in a variety of settings.

Much of the narrative that has accompanied this change, has seen an emphasis on our becoming more entrepreneurial, more innovative, and more creative to respond to the changes we are facing into the future.

As traditional industries have disappeared, options of working in low-paid sectors, with short-term or zero-hour contracts have very much become a reality, but if we don't want that or want something better, we will have to try and identify the 'next big thing' or carve out a niche for ourselves.

The reality though is this – not everyone can be an entrepreneur or innovator or inventor – we can't all be! Just like we can't all be famous, or successful or celebrities, we don't all have the capacity to develop new projects, products and so on.

And so, the question of why we push this agenda in such a way is worthy of much greater examination. My belief is that we have become stuck on a constant journey of exploring, designing, and producing endless shiny, sophisticated new tools or products, not only those of a physical kind, but tools of all varieties, e.g., methodologies, approaches, and models of practice, that we end up overlooking the more important things in life.

I have noticed the emergence or rather the re-emergence of patterns or traits – things that are re-forming, things repeating themselves, a recycling of previous ideas, and so on. We see it in the promotion of 'new' fitness regimes, in alternative (unproven) medicines, in lifestyle gurus promoting tailored messages about how you should live your life.

We see it in motivational classes and workshops about how you can fix your problems, in fresh approaches to growing, preparing, and cooking your own food, in digitialisation where there is a constant flow of new portals, platforms and tools for doing basically all the same essential things and so on – I think you get the picture!

Can you imagine if everyone was an entrepreneur where we would be constantly designing, developing, testing, promoting, and marketing new products – every one of us would be trying to sell each other variations of the same products. But then of course, one entrepreneur would simply say to another 'well I've got one already', whilst the other might then respond by saying 'sure, but mine does this'.

One of the contributing factors to this idea that everyone can or should be an entrepreneur or innovator, particularly in

Western society, is the capitalist system we grow up in. Schools prep us to be equipped to enter the labour market and continue to service this system. Now, it may seem a bit contradictory that I say this, because many would argue that all schools equip us to do effectively is take our place in the system, as if we are all part of the factory turnover of products being shipped out the door.

In his book *The Compassionate Mind*, Paul Gilbert writes, 'Every psychological study I know of actually says that, if you want to help children and adults, succeed and be confident, then focus on their efforts, not their results. Yet capitalism has no interest in our effort, only our result. '[18]

The point being that schools focus on results, and when you finish your secondary education, the choice is (give or take) to find work or go onto third level-education, but many of the jobs that traditionally existed, at least those that would give you a steady wage, are no longer there. And if you don't pursue university or college, and the jobs aren't there either, then the need to be innovative or entrepreneurial is greater than ever.

However, the skills that you might have needed to develop at school to be innovative or entrepreneurial do not exist, because you were merely following a curriculum that focuses only on results and testing only the things you can remember.

You leave school having developed the ability (more or less) to remember, without learning much needed essential skills for innovation to take your place in a world where jobs are often the 'gig economy' and many more have been replaced by automation, but in a parallel world, social media and reality TV tell you that you can fulfil your dreams if you only believe.

From a logical point of view, not everyone can be an entrepreneur or innovator, and not everyone wants to be. But there is a constant focus on these themes – from funding applications that seek new methods and approaches; from the Jobs & Benefits Office encouraging you to try a new career and re-invent yourself, to government policy telling you that you should be open to other professions and/or trying new jobs; from lots of bodies set up to help you start your own business, to educational institutions being entrepreneurial colleges, to innovation 'hubs' and incubation 'labs', to all sorts of publications pushing the entrepreneurial and innovation message.

By all means – encourage people to be innovative, creative, and entrepreneurial, but let's stop with this notion that everyone can be an entrepreneur or innovator.

10. There is never just one answer

He who has all the answers has not been asked all the questions.
Confucius

Judging by the way social media has evolved in recent years and its propensity to simply portray all manner of things in a simplistic black or white and right and wrong fashion, you could be forgiven if you simply thought there must be a right answer for everything. It's all too easy to assume from our limited knowledge that A = B when we draw our conclusions.

And who can really blame us? We might know how to construct a sentence, but just as a German friend stumped me many years ago when she asked me about the use of past participles in the English language, I never had to think about it until she asked me. When asked, and after a few seconds when the dazed look wore off me, I said, 'don't ask me about things like that, I only know how to speak the language.'

My point was that it's not something I thought about (or even think about now – perhaps it was one of those many days in school when I wasn't paying attention), because it was clear to me – I know how to speak the language – I don't really have to think that much about how the sentence is constructed.

I didn't have to, it was natural to me, I wasn't having to try and master a language that was fluent to me, and from memory, I could never recall this being a topic that was addressed when learning how to string a few words together or join letters into words at the tender age of five.

But that's exactly the problem – here was a German friend not only asking me for help to explain something that should be fundamental to me, but I wasn't even familiar with it, even though I'm fluent in the language. How can this be?

In some ways this is a metaphor for other life lessons – yes, we all know stuff, even if it isn't that well known to us, but how well do we know it? My German friend was being taught about another language and she was taught about the construction of that sentence using terminology I was wholly unfamiliar with. Wow! How did that happen?

Well, there is no clear answer, which in a sense is a metaphor for the metaphor – different education system, different teacher, different time, different person receiving the information and more besides.

Western culture contributes to this way of thinking – as Jesse J. Prinz describes: 'Western enthusiasm for logic is that Westerners tend to abide by the principle of non-contradiction: if two claims are conflicting, one of them must be false'[19] whereas in the East, there is an acceptance that more than one answer can be applicable to a particular question. This is what's more commonly known as 'duality'.

Amanda Gelter explains that 'two radically different theories might be dual to one another – that is, they might be two very different manifestations of the same underlying reality. Dualities are as counterintuitive a notion as they come, but physics is riddled with them'.[20]

Creativity guru Edward de Bono warns us of the danger of 'either/or polarisations because they suggest that the situation can only be looked at in these two ways'.[21]

The debate over this kind of thinking can be traced as far back as the seventeenth century when English philosopher Thomas Hobbes argued that human beings are naturally selfish only for a century later, when Jean-Jacques Rousseau argued that human beings are by their very nature peaceful and solitary.

Scotsman David Hume offered a third perspective suggesting that humans are naturally social and sympathetic to others. However, all of this ignores the idea that there is such variation in human behaviour, and this is often determined by the situation that people find themselves in, giving rise to the theory 'Situationism' which posits that behaviour is determined not by personal qualities but rather by circumstance.

Things might be clear to us as regards a wide range of issues, but the answer is anything but straightforward, hence why there is never just one answer. Social media has contributed to developing a narrative where questions usually only have one answer, and if I'm right, you must be wrong and vice versa. The brain has difficulty handling ambiguity, it is always looking for patterns and so individuals find it difficult comprehending things that do not make sense to them, hence a bias towards their own conclusions.

Social media encourages comments and not explanations, in part because our attention span is much shorter these days, and social media does not encourage us to explore answers or explanations but rather just respond to comments, and because we feel we are right, and even when we realise we are wrong, we feel compelled to defend the comments we have made because they represent us and if we change we look like we're not consistent, even though that is a bit of a daft notion, as we actually change all the time.

And with social media only designed to encourage short comments, we have an inherent capacity to be prone to errors, these often need context (which is most likely lacking), tone can be misinterpreted when someone disagrees, and there is an assumption that the intention of the other is to defend their position.

The reality is that there are many things we do not understand and nor can we – there is simply just too much to know. And when things confuse us, or don't look right, or appear suspicious, or don't meet our own loosely defined threshold for understanding, or because our brains are wired to look for patterns and we can't find them, we naturally assume that we can't be wrong, but rather the other person is, or conclusions reached by other sources must be wrong because it doesn't make sense to us.

Almost certainly in Western culture, we have been taught there has to be a right or wrong answer – there can be no in-between. This of course is misleading because, not everything is black or white, not everything is straightforward – many things have a variety of answers, not just one – there is never just one answer!

By the way, just in case you're wondering, 'a participle is a nonfinite verb form that has some of the characteristics and functions of both verbs and adjectives. More narrowly, participle has been defined as "a word derived from a verb and used as an adjective, as in a laughing face"'.[22]

11. There are no silver bullets

Thinking is difficult. That is why most people judge.
Carl Jung

Continuing in the same vein as the last lesson, I hasten to add that there are no silver bullets for anything. The term silver bullet is essentially a metaphor for a simple, seemingly magical, solution to a difficult or complex problem.

We have seen this most vividly during the Covid pandemic, when, for example, 'anti-vaxxers' in their opposition to vaccines almost ironically, argued (through their own reactions to vaccines) that vaccines themselves were supposed to be a 'silver bullet' but turned out not to be and therefore had no credibility and therefore their anti-vaccine stance was justified.

Vaccines, of course, were developed to respond to Covid, but as new strains of Covid appeared and responded in-kind, anti-vaxxers were at pains to point out that they didn't work and therefore no one should take them.

The irony is, of course, that no one said that vaccines were the *be-all-end-all* and most certainly not the magic bullet that anti-vaxxers would have you believe was promised by the scientific community.

There may have been moments when politicians (sometimes in an effort to demonstrate their commitment to vaccines, or articulate their merits), spoke without really thinking, as oft they do, but at no point did those involved in the development of vaccines say they had created the silver bullet, not ever!

Those involved were at pains to point out the various efficacy rates (performance under ideal controlled conditions) of vaccines but none of them ever stated they were 100% effective. Nor did they guarantee you wouldn't catch Covid let alone defeat it but rather they made clear that their effectiveness was in reducing not only transmission levels and your chances of dying if you became ill, but also becoming hospitalised, or ending up in ICU (Intensive Care Unit). Again, they were keen to point out that vaccines were only one of several 'tools' in the fight against Covid.

I have always found it ironic that it is the anti-vaxxers, in their vehement opposition to vaccines, that want to ensure the impression that those involved in the development of vaccines were the ones that promised us the 'all-singing, all-dancing' solution to Covid.

Because the wider scientific community were challenged by the evolution of differing mutations, the anti-vaxxers are keen to assert that the *all-singing, all-dancing* vaccine never worked anyways and therefore we shouldn't take them, especially after boosters have been introduced – as if this was also some kind of broken promise because one or two jabs wouldn't cut it! That's the equivalent of a doctor saying to a cancer patient, 'listen that first dose of radiography didn't work, we'll just have to call it a day, because if one dose doesn't work, no chance of a second doing the job.'

Somehow, they managed to turn it into a narrative about how the collective efforts of the scientific community to wrestle with a deadly invisible enemy were futile because one dose didn't work, almost as if to suggest that the virus might say to itself, 'you know what, I'll just head on home, I've toyed with you enough, I've had my fun, I'm going to stop now.'

What is clear from Covid and is a warning to us all, is that there really isn't a 'silver bullet' and that solutions to challenges that we face are complex, often very nuanced and anything but black and white. There is no one challenge we face in the current era that has a straightforward answer; everything is nuanced, everything is grey.

To have a greater appreciation of the nuances and complexities involved in not only developing vaccines but more generally, how life per se functions, we need to take an interest in an area that we rarely think about – microbes. They don't get much attention but in an essay by Stewart Brand, 'Microbes run the world', he points out that 'in 1/5 of a teaspoon of sea water, there are a million bacteria (and 10 million viruses)... The human microbiome in our gut, mouth, skin and elsewhere, harbour three thousand kinds of bacteria with 3 billion distinct genes'.[23]

I was somewhat surprised by the reaction of many to the news that we were hit by a pandemic – or to put it more succinctly, I was surprised that people were surprised. We humans are quite vulnerable and reflecting on the practices we have developed over time, e.g., development of chemical weapons, use of pesticides, industrial farming, poor regulations in food production among many other questionable practices, my view always has been that something has to give.

With each new virus that has appeared, humans have had to evolve their own immunity in response, but for many millennia, and long before scientific and medical minds (among others) sought to find answers and responses to the many diseases we have faced, humanity was extremely vulnerable.

Covid has proven that we are still very much at risk and particularly susceptible no matter how sophisticated we think we might be. For example, William Davies and Jonathan Cape in their book, *Nervous States, How Feeling Took Over the World*, warn that, 'The use of antibiotics in farming, combined with improper disposal of agricultural waste, is creating swamps filled with antibiotics in which new strains of "superbug" can develop' and had previously estimated that by 2017 'the number of people dying due to drug-resistant infections was around 700, 000 a year globally but current trends suggest this will rise to 10 million a year by 2050'.[23]

The notion of a silver bullet is almost entirely myth. Our ability to address a wide variety of challenges is much more nuanced and complex than we like to admit. Take, for example, the subject of predictions. We all think we are pretty good with predictions, or at least we tend to convince ourselves, retrospectively, that we are.

As mentioned in Lesson Three, Philip Tetlock evaluated 28, 361 predictions from nearly 300 self-appointed professionals and discovered that their ability to make successful predictions was on a par with a 'dart-throwing chimpanzee'. As almost every fact of life depends on predictions, or projections even, which we have seen is a feature of daily briefings on Covid, this highlights vividly that the existence a silver bullet is simply an exaggeration at best and at worst, a complete falsehood. If anyone should ever try to simplify an issue, take a moment to remind them that 'dart-throwing chimpanzee' might have been more successful than someone that considers him or herself an expert.

12. Don't expect people to change if there is no change at any level

You change your life by changing your heart.
Dreamstime.com

Over the years I have gotten into lots of discussions, debates, and arguments. I must confess I have enjoyed them and have been drawn to them somehow, for a variety of reasons, which I suspected was probably grounded in some egotistical desire to be proven right when I was younger, because of course being right is good, right? Wrong! Sometimes, but of course not always. In fact, it's good to be wrong at times – that's where real learning can come from. I'm not sure where that desire to be right came from though, whether it's informed by my upbringing or is in my DNA so to speak, or a combination of both.

As I have got older and 'wiser', I have (at times) struggled with trying not to get drawn into discussions and arguments, knowing full well that once I'm in, I'm in! I think a contributing factor to my approach is that my being a youth worker by profession leads me to stick to the conviction that we must challenge prejudice, assumptions, hatred and broad generalisations about people and things if it is not founded in fact or reality.

There's a price to pay for that, the perception that I'm argumentative, stubborn, or provocative, but I also believe that you subscribe to challenging these things because if you don't, nobody learns, and, more broadly, people learn not to be accountable or not to assume responsibility for their words and actions.

I've had to learn over the years to pick my battles and reconcile myself with the idea that it is okay not to challenge everything! In a world besieged with the notion (or it certainly appears so) that feelings equal truth and opinion equals evidence, there is, however, a need to challenge many of the assumptions or generalisations that swirl around us.

What I have discovered (at least in my own humble estimation) that whilst this is an admirable approach, because to challenge can create opportunities for learning, what has become patently clear, though, is that many people do not want to change, that their opinion or idea(s) are fixed, and no end of effort to persuade individuals no matter how strong the evidence is will not achieve the desired outcome.

To persuade people means they must review what they stand for and if they have put a lot of time and energy into the position they hold, this is almost nothing short of impossible. It usually results from transformational events, and even then, people can still be in denial. As Daniel Kahneman tells us, 'We pay more attention to the content of messages than to information about their reliability, and as a result end up with a view of the world around us that is simpler and more coherent than the data justify.'[25]

Persuading others to change means individuals having to reflect on the things that constitute their identity, and this can mean a process of 'undressing themselves in public', where they have to unpeel layers and in effect, years of (sometimes carefully formed) beliefs, values, principles, etc., which are often bound up in their upbringing and background, and means that they might have to re-write their history or many of the stories they know and hold close to their heart.

I have learned over the years that if people struggle with the smallest of change, they will struggle with bigger change, especially if it's 'forced'. Another thing I've learned is not that I should expect others to change, but that I need to tailor my own expectations of them – it's me that must change and adapt, not them. It's my own expectations and hopes for others that needs reviewing. This can of course be frustrating, especially if you know that they have the propensity to change, to reflect, or to take on board new information, but still just plainly refuse to even consider it.

David Mc Rainey offers insight into why this is – 'your opinions are the result of years of paying attention to information that confirmed what you believed, while ignoring information that challenged your preconceived notions... his research [Valdis Krebs] shows what psychological research into confirmation bias predicts: you want to be right about how you see the world, so you seek out information that confirms your beliefs and avoid contradictory evidence and opinions'.[26]

I found this during the 'Covid years', when friends, acquaintances, and family were expressing various opinion across a range of subjects. I engaged in discussion and was sometimes amazed at what they would share, often from completely unreliable and biased sources, often mere opinion and not grounded in any semblance of reality or fact, and I would 'engage' them, commenting on their posts or their broad generalisations.

I challenged them because I couldn't accept posts that they shared on social media were truly reflective of them, or their values and beliefs. I believed that there was more to them than that which they were sharing, and that they had much greater capacity to think critically about the subject they were expressing their opinion on, or in many cases not sharing an opinion on, but rather sharing someone else's.

Unfortunately, I was to discover they were not willing or able to change, and even the smallest critique of their opinion led to my excommunication (at least in social media terms). I've even had some relatives 'unfriend' me as a result!

So be prepared, know that by challenging anyone you are (potentially) incurring the wrath of individuals, and there is no right or wrong answer as it were, only a response, one that has implications.

Even a mere exchange of views these days can result in a torrent of abuse, even if you are trying to merely highlight a contradiction, or a flaw in the argument that they propose, which in many cases can be one that belongs to someone else, but of course reinforces their own opinion.

Understand that if people struggle with change on a small scale, e.g., a change to their daily routines, a reaction to innocuous comments and so on, then don't expect large-scale change; that change is reserved for you, the change being that you have to accept that you can't change them, most certainly not by 'force', even if you were only debating an issue with them.

13. The need to be aware of reality, accept it but still believe that change is possible

We should be lifting each other up and cheering each other on, not trying to outshine one another. The sky would be awfully dark with just one star.

Brightvibes

As a Youth Worker by profession (have I said that already? Sorry!), there is one internal battle that I have to accept but never have been really able to reconcile – I believe in the power of what I do and the ability to bring transformational change to the lives of young people but I know deep down that no matter how committed, or willing, or determined to ensure change, there are just some young people that I cannot 'save', and when I say save, I don't mean in some spiritual or faith-based way.

I use the term 'save' metaphorically of course, and don't know for one second, if I have 'saved' anyone before. I have those 'magic moments' when people come up to me or even out of the blue call to thank me for things that I have done, moments I created, or opportunities I presented to them, and this is beautiful to hear. I don't go looking for it, but I'll concede, it's very nice when I hear it – it just makes it worthwhile that you are making a difference.

I know that it cannot or could not always be like this, but in all the situations I enter, be it with young people, my children, friends, and so on, I do so on the basis that I believe that change is possible, that I can help make a difference and that my contributions or efforts will not be wasted.

To give my chosen profession validity and a sense of credibility, in my own mind at least, I must keep believing that this aspiration I hold still rings true because it gives me hope, it allows me to dream, to imagine, and to create possibilities.

It's the choice between positive and negative, can do and cannot do, light and dark, and gives me motivation to carry on and keeps my faith in humanity and its ability to redeem itself intact.

It extends beyond the boundaries of my profession of course, not only as part of my internal belief system but also an eternal belief in the potential of human nature, that it can be more than it is often perceived or how it appears in the present era; that it can be care, compassion, kindness, solidarity, co-operation and empathy over apathy, insensitivity, indifference, hatred, competition, and individualism.

Accepting the reality of situations we observe or sometimes find ourselves in, where we witness or hear of people, bodies or government departments for example, behaving towards individuals with at best indifference or at worst with a callous disregard is hard to fathom, because we have this idea that people should observe the 'golden rule' (or the many variations of it) where people treat each other as they might expect to be treated themselves.

That of course assumes that everyone has grown up with that (particular) notion or have been surrounded with individuals who share that ideal or have experienced environments that are marked out with kindness, compassion or at least a degree of sensitivity that leads them to consider the thoughts and feelings of others, but as we know, this is often not the case. People are the result of their experiences, and if they grow up into an environment without these qualities, then they know no different, and will behave in a manner that only they are familiar with.

Paul Gilbert tells us that 'our sense of what is right and wrong is related to complex interactions between genetic disposition, learning, conformity, learned social values, "feelings" of things and reasoning'.[28]

I still want to believe that change is possible, because the alternative is to believe it's not, and therefore means choosing not to make any effort with individuals that might otherwise respond positively to their being shown some patience, kindness, sensitivity and even love.

In some ways it's understandable that not everyone can be on the same page with this idea of what can be described as an altruistic society. Not everyone grows up into an experience where they have the security of loving parents or at least supportive adults in their life or that they haven't survived some form of trauma whether that be bereavement, divorce, or abuse, among others. Let's be honest, life is difficult. There's a lot to enjoy, admire and appreciate but as Pankaj Mishra testifies,

we live today in a vast, homogenous world market, in which human beings are programmed to maximise their self-interest and aspire to the same things, regardless of their difference of cultural background and individual temperament. The world seems more literate, interconnected and prosperous than at any other time in history. Average well-being has risen, if not equitably; economic misery has been alleviated in even the poorest parts of India and China. There has been a new scientific revolution marked by 'artificial' intelligence, robotics, drones, the mapping of the human genome, genetic manipulation and cloning, deeper exploration of space, and fossil fuels from fracking. But the promised universal civilisation – one harmonized by a combination of universal suffrage, broad educational opportunities, steady economic growth, and private initiative and personal advancement – has not materialised.[29]

I accept that there are indeed people in the world that are unkind, indifferent, lack the capacity for caring and have no reason to display any kind of solidarity to another human being, but they weren't born that way, and with a bit of empathy and compassion, they might find a way to regain or learn even, some of the traits of humanity that mark us out as different.

The world is challenging, there are so many demands on us from being different to being something, something more than we can conceivably manage, where expectations are great, and where one slip or indiscretion is punished unrelentingly in the court of public opinion, and therefore it's not surprising as everyone strives to make it, or even just to survive.

It seems we live in an era where solidarity is sorely lacking but we have been led to believe that humans are fundamentally selfish, or at least uncooperative, that it's in their nature to be competitive and not to look out for each other. Research in recent years has shown this to be untrue, and the opposite is true. Even if we doubt this, we still must have faith in humanity's capacity for change.

14. It's too easy to say that people are dumb, even if it appears like it – so let's not

When you debate a person about something that affects them more than it affects you, remember that it will take a much greater emotional toll on them than you. For you it may feel like an Academic Exercise. For them it feels like revealing their pain only to have you dismiss their experience and sometimes their humanity. The fact that you might remain more calm under these circumstances is a consequence of your privilege, not increased objectivity on your part. Stay humble.
@happyvulcan

It is far too easy to give into that instinctive temptation that often befalls us and say people are dumb when they don't get the point we are making or even if it just feels like it. Let's face it, we wouldn't be human if we haven't done this at some point, even if we managed to conceal it from our facial expression or managed to avoid uttering those very words.

It's quite possible they have never been taught, or encouraged to think more broadly, nor driven to consider other possibilities, or even contemplate answers outside of their worldview. Therefore, anyone not benefitting from this kind of learning lacks the capacity to understand as opposed to not being able to think. They demonstrate a lack of empathy towards an issue that is important to you or towards an individual or a group of people that you might know, rather than not caring because they themselves might not have been encouraged to think or feel this way. This is why storytelling is so important, to hear at firsthand people's lived experience.

Stephen M. Kosslyn puts it another way, 'in short, each of us grows as we age and experience more and varied situations and ideas... what we understand about ourselves depends on what we paid attention to at the time events unfolded and on our imperfect conceptual machinery for interpreting ourselves'.[30]

What I refer to as the 'Covid Times', (no, not a newspaper) or the Covid era (which at the time of writing has only been replaced in the headlines by the war in Ukraine), which does imply an end point, although I don't think it will actually end as such, more a case of it being carefully managed until it runs its course and loses potency, or we develop more robust responses – will be looked back upon as one of extremes when the story of Covid comes to be written.

From those that followed all the rules, restrictions and lockdowns to those that steadfastly refused to even accept that Covid existed; from those that wore masks out of the notion of solidarity with people they didn't know to those that refused in the belief they were upholding the principle of choice and protecting their freedoms; from those that stood with BLM (Black Lives Matter) to those that labelled it as a terrorist movement; from those that protested the existence of statues and monuments and tore them down to those that fought to retain them and defend them irrespective of their history or significance; the latter years of the second decade of the twenty-first century, and early years of the third decade, will be remembered for much of the division that has emerged.

That division seems to have gathered momentum with events like BREXIT, followed quickly by the election of Donald Trump as President of the United States. That coupled with emergence and cementing of several 'hard man' leaders including Putin, Orbán, Modi, and Bolsonaro, all with very conservative and right-leaning mindsets, clearly indicates that this cultural and political divergence has been in the pipeline for some time.

However, and what is striking, particularly in the UK and US, is the level of inarticulation among both Trump and BREXIT Supporters. Whether it's baseless claims, conspiracy theories or mere opinion, a distinguishing feature is at times arguments laden with irony, contradiction and confusion, arguments that often deflect from the real issue or are conflated with other issues, and those that are often imagined or exaggerated. We've all seen the videos uploaded online – incoherent, inarticulate, and contradictory, from those that appear to have little or no real understanding of the issue that they seem to be protesting about, the temptation is (and I must confess I have done it myself), to laugh but this was more an older habit but even when I did, I realised that this a little dismissive and belittles what for many are genuine concerns.

What saddens me in as much as it frustrates me, is the inability of those protesting to articulate any seemingly cohesive argument to support their claims. Most appear to come from traditionally white working-class areas – they appear as soundbites as if held up to be reflective of a wider yet ignorant working-class consensus.

At times it's painful to watch, but in all honesty it's actually quite sad, because behind those snippets and soundbites is something more concerning – aside from fear, frustration and the sense of abandonment (and, of course, this is mixed with a sense of entitlement bestowed upon areas that serviced 'Empire' and the 'Land of the Free') most keenly felt in white working-class areas, is a distinct lack of understanding of what are often very complex and nuanced issues, and which are not anything near as black and white as they are often portrayed.

And that for me is the saddest part of all – populations that have been done a disservice because the education system in which they grew up taught them only to remember 'stuff' and failed to equip them with the capacity to think critically about issues they face or have experienced. June Sarpong underlines this when she points out that, '70 per cent of those with only GCSEs or less voted to leave the EU and 67 per cent of non-college-educated white voters ticked for Trump.'[31] These figures are stark and should signal a warning. All of this makes me think of a line in the song 'The Island' by Paul Brady – regarding how ordinary people may not understand the facts of a given situation – which epitomises (for me) what it means to be working class. Many of the other lines convey the story of 'the Troubles' in Northern Ireland which has by far disproportionately affected those in working-class communities.

The working class (you see) were busy working – access to higher and further education was out of reach, and thus the possibility of mixing in diverse circles, and critiquing their own thoughts and reflections and those of others was missed, and so many of the wars – literal and metaphorical – historical and current – political, cultural or otherwise, are often played out by those where access to education and the opportunity for meaningful participation in educational discourse beyond primary and secondary level is denied, or at least inaccessible.

And then we see the results turning up in the snippets and soundbites on TV, Radio and online, and collectively we laugh, dismiss, or look down upon them, yet they are only reflective of the system that they grew up into but did not have the opportunity to move beyond. And in societies where further and higher education costs too much to take part in, this will remain so. Of course, there is a school of thought that suggests that it's deliberately kept like this, i.e., don't educate the masses or they'll rise up! Yet for many, they are already angry! It's easy to laugh and dismiss the inarticulate, those that can't pull together a cohesive sentence never mind argument, those that seemingly flock to join or support movements or causes without appearing to know why, yet this is what the state has produced. It's not funny, it is genuinely sad. So, resist the temptation to say people are dumb. Stay humble!

15. Daydreaming is our natural state of mind, our default position, and it isn't a bad thing

Scientists have discovered that it takes approximately 400 repetitions to create a new synapse in the brain, unless it is done in play, in which case it only takes 10 to 20 repetitions.

Karen Purvis

(Little Pine Learning)

I think it's fair to say that we've all grown up hearing the expression, 'stop daydreaming', or at least something akin to this, most probably during our time at school. We've all found ourselves on the receiving end of the teacher's ire when our mind drifts and we're looking out the window or staring passively ahead and thinking about any matter of things other than what the teacher was talking about or asking us to consider.

Unless the subject was captivating or the style of teaching was engaging, we've all had those moments when daydreaming was part of our school experience – most probably our everyday school experience. As adults we still daydream or as I like to call it these days, *drifting*, where our mind goes a wandering. Be that in the shower, whilst driving or sitting in a meeting, and so on, we drift continuously.

There is something soothing and calming about drifting – we don't try to monitor our thinking, we don't discern, we don't discriminate, we just let our thoughts roam free. We know they are safe in our minds and there they stay unless we decide to share them.

We have grown up, however, with the notion that daydreaming is a bad thing – teachers would define it as not being able to concentrate, whilst parents would often dismiss us as ignoring them. The reality is that daydreaming is good, it's our natural state, it's where many of our most effective thoughts come from, and the key thing is that it's not a bad state to be in. Much research has been completed over the years that tells us that daydreaming is that state of mind which comes most naturally to us.

'In the see saw of attention, Western culture overvalues the central executive mode, and undervalues the daydreaming mode. The central executive approach to problem-solving is often diagnostic analytic, and impatient, whereas daydreaming approach is playful, intuitive, and relaxed'[32] writes Daniel J. Levitin.

This is further exacerbated by children always having to be 'switched on'. Robert Colville explains that children have quite limited time to play these days – 'for today's children, their spare time is over-structured, packed with extra lessons and activities. That's not just because parents are desperate to spur their development – it's also because they're frightened of letting them fly free.... It's the friendships, not the devices, that matter to them.... And, why aren't they out there meeting in person?'[33]

To maximise our creativity, we need to be able to imagine, but imagination is not something that is readily nurtured in our lives. Much of our imagination can be found in our natural state of daydreaming, but how often as a child, or even as a young person, have we been told to stop doing exactly that – sit up straight, stop dreaming, be realistic, focus, stop your mind wandering sort of thing.

At school, we are conditioned only to remember things and then to recite them when called upon and being punished when we can't. Then we go onto a college where maybe for the first time, we must think for ourselves, but we're directed to the library to find answers in books that are usually locked away in someone's bedroom. Then as a result, if we come up with alternative theories to show our creative side we are inevitably marked down because we exceeded the remit given to us.

If it's not college, we go into jobs where we are expected to fulfil a role, an expectation already determined for us – a job with very little space for trial and error. Perhaps we don't go into that job but rather 'sign on' at 'the dole' or whatever the equivalent of the unemployment office where you are, and proceed to slowly fall into a rut, where much of our potential for creativity is lost whilst we wait for our big break.

Or we decide, screw it all – we're going to be an entrepreneur or innovator, or what's now often referred to as a disruptor, only to realise that most entrepreneurial efforts don't succeed. Boom! And before we know it, we're well into our 20s trying to imagine what our future looks like because we have always been taught that the future is a period of time far in the distance, rather than even looking at the future as almost immediate, in that in order to get to the future, we need to create the changes or make the plans now.

We dismiss daydreaming and do not stress enough the importance of creativity and imagination. We see every health remedy in tablet form, we have advisers, gurus, and leaders for every facet of our lives, and we view everything as marketable products. Above all, we believe our way is the best way to do things.

It's essential that daydreaming is indeed understood to be a very natural part of our make-up and is conducive to imagining, and not limited to those who are most vocal or speak most often. 'Creativity engages the brain's daydreaming mode forging links between concepts and neural nodes that might not otherwise be made. Time stops. We contemplate. We reimagine our relationship to the world.'[34]

When we drift, we tend not to be cognisant of the thoughts that normally constrain us. There's a certain kind of flow as we freely bounce from one thought to another, often random, at times making no sense but amounting to a moment where we do not focus on the thoughts that perhaps bring the normal stresses that we are more accustomed to.

Daydreaming allows us to play with our thoughts as it were by not imposing boundaries and allowing us to enter a state of mind where there are no boundaries. If we allow ourselves more space and time to do exactly that, we can also allow our 'creative juices' to flow and thus nurture a greater sense of imagination.

The world we are in right now demands much greater imagination to address the challenges we face. As Greg Lukianoff and Jonathon Haidt tell us 'we will all have to exercise enormous creativity and imagination in order to see and understand what is happening around us and work out new solutions to the problems that now face us, recognizing both the opportunities and the dangers ahead'.[35]

As Einstein once said, 'Logic will get you from A to B. Imagination will take you everywhere.' If we want to get anywhere, we should begin with daydreaming.

16. Good behaviours are just as contagious as bad

Rather fail with honour than succeed by fraud.
Sophocles

In the current era you'd be forgiven for thinking that only bad news makes headlines – I think it's a fair assertion that it's most probably true. Several journalists I have got to know down the years have essentially told me this themselves – good news is not sexy and thus the focus on the negative, the controversial and the contentious gets primetime.

With vast technological change in the last 10–20 years, we have moved from thrice-daily news bulletins (basically lunch, dinner, and night-time) to rolling 24-7 news not only through what was our main source of news – the TV – but to all manner of technology, most notably our mobile phones.

The impact of this, of course, is that we have news at our fingertips and on demand and if we are surrounded by what appears to be negative news, then the impression it leaves is that everything is negative, and everyone is behaving badly, or at least without due consideration to others.

I use my laptop daily, and I've observed language and terminology used to describe things in this era that I would say comes close to volatile. Every time I open a tab on my browser MSN appears and a plethora of news stories, page after page, all of which use language to catch our attention. Catching our attention of course is normal, an old marketing trick as it were, but even I can say with confidence that it's no longer just the 'front page' anymore but almost all articles that appear online aside from those generated by media outlets such as *The Independent*, *The Guardian*, *Financial Times* and *Reuters*.

Let me offer an example – every news story on the main headline banner has an element of drama about it – of course this has often been the case in the media – but it's the terminology that is used these days that seems to enforce this impression – 'warning', 'forced', 'apocalyptic', 'fatal', 'devastated', and 'permanently damage' are just a smattering of current headline-grabbing stories as I write this. The discourse is often reactionary, judgemental, conflictual, and designed to antagonise, so it wouldn't come as a shock if indeed it feels like everyone is at loggerheads.

Thankfully, just in the same way that bad behaviour is contagious, we also know that good behaviour is equally contagious. People mirror the words and actions of one another and so if you adopt a tone or approach which is designed to de-escalate then it is likely that people will follow and if people go out of their way to show empathy, kindness, care, and compassion, we know that this is likely to be reciprocated. There is plenty of evidence to demonstrate this.

Douglas Rushkoff writes that, 'We've been conditioned to believe in the myth that evolution is about competition: the survival of the fittest.... By viewing evolution through a strictly competitive lens, we miss the bigger story of our own social development and have trouble understanding humanity as one big, interconnected team.'[36]

Rutger Bregman points to 'more human skills like empathy, self-regulation, conscientiousness, teamwork, resilience, problem-solving, innovation and critical thinking-skills'[37] that will ensure a more successful life, whilst Jesse J. Prinz, asserts that 'human success depends on cooperation. We enter trade agreements, build collective works, form treaties, establish enduring social bonds, farm together and raise kids together. Almost everything we do depends on cooperation, and, without it, we'd be back in the cave, or worse'. The challenge we face though is what Henry Timms and Jeremy Heimans argue that 'new power can supercharge hate and misinformation'.[38]

We have already seen how those traditional forms of power, i.e., parliamentary politics can supercharge hate and misinformation with clever use of social media, Donald Trump being an obvious example. But equally, companies like Facebook which can be described as one of the new powers has largely washed its hands of its responsibility for supercharging hate and misinformation.

The same for Twitter and it's only been because both are being forced by Governments either side of the Atlantic to address these concerns has it begun to take its responsibility seriously. Both companies have historically tried to argue their position as being one of only providing the means by which information is hosted but not actually responsible for the formulation of content itself – a bit like saying we make guns and ammunition but not responsible for who uses it and for what purpose; also similar to politicians that use all sorts or rhetoric against a particular minority but when a supporter uses violence against that minority, they then do a *Pontus Pilate* and wash their collective hands of responsibility

Amazon which alongside Apple and Facebook are among the *Big Five*, and all of whom possess greater economic power than countless states combined, is as famous for its reputation as a poor employer as it is for its services.

'Good behaviours are just as contagious as bad. Organisations that allow employees to ignore ethics form a breeding ground for bad behaviour that tempts even the most ethically minded and strong-willed person'[39] asserts Daniel J. Levitin. At the time of writing, the British Government led by Boris Johnston is facing a major crisis – *Party Gate* – over the allegation that it held numerous parties during Covid, whist the country was in lockdown – the words of Levitin in this case ring true.

It would have only taken one party to happen to give the green light to the rest – not as a conscious decision as such (although as the evidence in this case seems to suggest it very much was a conscious decision) but rather something along the lines of, 'sure another one won't do any harm' or like the expression goes, 'hung for a sheep as hung for a lamb'.

Once you cross that line there is no going back, and sure, then it doesn't really matter how many times you cross the line in a manner of speaking. Equally, not crossing that line means you deliver a different kind of message, behaviour that is acceptable, behaviour that is honourable, behaviour that demonstrates a commitment to upholding values that are reflective of care, compassion, generosity, kindness, and solidarity among others.

The expression 'mob psychology' springs to mind, where bad behaviour spreads like a wildfire among 'the crowd' but as we have seen with Covid, where communities looked out for each other, particularly the most vulnerable, good behaviour is also contagious, and more of us are good than bad.

17. Too much information is a bad thing

If you ever want evidence that the world's a terrible place, watch the news and surf the web. But if you want to remember how incredible this planet is, go into the nature. Unlike social media and the news, nature has no incentive to keep us agitated, angry or anxious.

Austin Perlmutter

It is somewhat illogical as a certain Chief Science Officer might say, but as it turns out the more information we have, the worse we are at decision-making. Research has shown that we need a certain level of information to make credible decisions but if we are in receipt of too much information, our ability to make decisions and good decisions at that weakens.

We live in an era when we have more than enough information to make positive and well-informed decisions, yet the evidence is that our ability to do so has lessened. According to Levitin, 'The number of possessions the average person has now is far greater than we've had for most of our evolutionary history by a factor of 1000.'[40] That of course is different to information but if our possessions have increased by a factor of 1000, can you imagine how much information we now take in compared with just a couple of decades ago, never mind that of our ancestors.

Let's explore possessions for a moment – buying one possession can take us quite some time, not least of all because there are so many more things to consider. Take, for example, a car – when my father was buying a car, it really came down to what you could afford and with that in mind, what was on offer, and perhaps fuel costs including how economical the car was. You might have preferred a particular make and model but largely it was simply a choice of affordability – and it was either hatch, saloon, or estate.

Now the variety of shape these days has changed immensely – the above plus cross-overs, MPVs, SUV and so on. Even the size of engine – it was usually 1300 or 1600, and petrol or diesel. Even how you purchased the car in the past was fairly straightforward – cash! Now there are all sorts of arrangements. Of course, there's nothing wrong with this but it just means a lot more thought about decisions that were historically straightforward.

When I was younger, going to the shop to buy a packet of crisps was simple – Cheese and Onion, Salt 'n' Vinegar, Ready Salted and Prawn Cocktail. I'd be the first to welcome greater choice bearing in mind that Salt 'n' Vinegar and Ready Salted was for me like choosing between a rock and a hard place – it had the same level of flavour, so Cheese and Onion or Prawn Cocktail were really the only choices going. Nearly forgot – Smokey Bacon – although that flavour was a bit like the cousin that's invited to a wedding out of courtesy!

The world we occupy now is vastly different from the one we occupied only a few decades ago – why? Well in the main, because of information. We live in a world where we have not only incredible access to information but at a touch of a button, or rather the touch of a screen.

It's amazing, astonishing in fact, not least because as someone who worked in 'Youth Information' in the late '80s and early '90s, how I used to answer queries from those coming through the door was so different as to be almost archaic.

Andre Lih makes the point that the nature of how we communicate information has changed because 'while we are generating content and connections that are feeding a rich global conversation unimaginable just ten years ago, we may have no way to re-create, reference, research, and study this information after the fact.... Twitter, in particular, has emerged as the heart of a new global public conversation'.[41]

Of course, whilst new technologies and means of communication are welcome, the flip side brings with it a whole other side that is not so becoming. Noga Arikha talks about how we are living in an age of 'information glut, not deep knowledge'[42] whilst Herbert Simpson describes how 'a wealth of information creates a poverty of attention'.[43]

Another side-effect of the age of information is our level of patience. Nicholas G. Carr warns that 'every time a network gets quicker, we become antsier. As we experience faster flows of information online, we become, in other words, less patient people'.[44]

Tania Lombrozo adds a further layer of warning that, 'It follows that smarter and more efficient information retrieval via machines could foster dumber and less effective information-processing in human minds... People suffer from illusions of understanding... current trends toward faster, easier, and more seamless information retrieval threaten to exacerbate rather than correct any misplaced confidence in what we truly comprehend.'[45]

Michael Vassar talks about information warfare – 'News, as a concept, is gone. Science, as a concept, is gone. In information warfare, the assumption that reliable, low-context communication is even possible recedes into fantasy, taking with it both news and science and replacing them with politics and marketing.'[46]

This information warfare that Vassar describes is further exacerbated by what has become known as echo chambers that we share with 'like-minded' people, where 'we hear this message over and over... things posted by the friends you care about are higher up in your News Feed... Sociologists describe the innate tendency to associate and connect with people similar to us as homophily... The algorithm tweak means we are limiting our exposure to opposing perspectives'.[47]

At a macro level, our systems of governance are at risk from their over-reliance on information – 'humanity's future selective pressures appear likely to remain tied to economic theory that uses as its central construct a market model based on assumption of perfect information'.[48]

Information has also been presented in another way – how we are all in need of being fixed. We have so many choices to make now and so many proposed solutions – Rutger Bregman gives an insight into some of the modern choices we must make: 'we go to a doctor when we're sick, a therapist when we're sad, a dietitian when we're overweight, a prison when we're convicted, and a job coach when we're out of work'.[49]

What are we to do with all this new information? Whilst we need information, what is clear is that too much information can leave us overwhelmed and struggling to function if not indeed barely functioning.

18. Although it is important to respect other points of view, not all are equally valid

Please stop saying you 'researched it.'

You didn't research anything and its highly probable that you don't even know how to do so.

Did you compile a literature review and write abstracts on each article? Or better yet, did you collect a random sample of sources and perform independent probability statistics on the reported results? No?

Did you at least take each article, one by one and look into the sources (that would be the author, publisher and funder) then critique the writing for logical fallacies, cognitive distortions and plain inaccuracies.

Did you ask yourself why this source might publish these particular results? Did you follow the trail of references and apply the same source of scrutiny to them?

No? Then you didn't research fucking anything. You read or watched a video, with little objectivity. You came across something in your algorithm manipulated feed, something that jived with your implicit biases and served your confirmation bias, and subconsciously applied your emotional filters and called it proof.

Scary.
Linda Gamble Spadaro

A common mistake, one that is often played out in the media, is where all opinions are equally valid. I subscribe to the notion that people are entitled to their opinion but the idea that we give equal weighting or provide oxygen to certain opinions is dangerous. Let me explain. If for example, you give airtime to those that still believe the earth is flat, or that those born disabled is attributed to the 'sins of the past', well, this is just plainly wrong.

The days of questioning whether humans are responsible for climate change is long past, but if you are organising a television debate about climate change and give equal time to those that deny the overwhelming evidence that demonstrates this, again this is plainly wrong, as you are just adding to disinformation that already exists. As Susan Cain asserts, 'Everyone is entitled to their own opinions but not their own facts.'[50]

Some years ago, I was on a training programme about Risk Awareness, which was exploring Child Protection and Safeguarding. A conversation came up around paedophilia, and one of the participants – who was coming from outside the UK and a from country where there was quite a different culture towards issues around sex and gender, and a culture where a lot of misogynistic attitudes still exist – expressed an opinion, that sex between an adult and a minor (an adolescent in this case) was not paedophilia if it was consensual.

As you can imagine it caused a bit of a stir and so a discussion ensued. Even though we respected the individual and were appreciative of his honesty (even though it was a little bit surprising to say the least), it was not an issue we could compromise on even if it might have been out of respect for the guy just because he was entitled to his opinion.

Given the country he was coming from and culture that exists there, it was perhaps understandable why he might have had this opinion – it was a strongly conservative country, where

Female Genital Mutilation and arranged marriages still took place in some areas, and sex was a taboo subject.

That was no reasonable excuse for any of us to bestow any kind of legitimacy upon his beliefs – they were rightly challenged and in fairness to him he did listen to what we had to say but whether it made any lasting difference I have no idea. The training programme was only 4–5 days long and I haven't seen him since.

On another occasion I was day-tripping with a friend after a meeting in Slovenia. She very kindly agreed to show me parts of the area I was staying in. A conversation came up during the journey about immigrants and it was clear she had certain views (none of which I knew she held until then) and went as far as joking about Hitler being right.

These are the kind of moments when I must hold myself back. Rather than reacting, I prefer to use the opportunity to challenge opinion of that nature but without isolating the person. As we know only too well, you attack the person, there is only one outcome, so the importance of focusing on the subject and not the person is vital.

Even though I got on very well with the person concerned and was quite fond of her, I could not stand by and not challenge her opinion. Again, another moment when that person is entitled to her opinion (no matter how abhorrent I think it is) but it is not only not equally valid, but it also simply has no validity at all.

Just because we believe in the notion or the idea that people are entitled to an opinion, does not mean that all opinions are equal, or even that some have any kind of validity, especially those that are entirely without evidence. I'm not talking about two football fans debating which team is more successful, or which striker is better and so on.

Richard Dawkins describes how if schools taught the double-blind control experiment our cognitive toolkits would be much improved as we would 'learn not to generalise from anecdotes... we would learn how to assess the likelihood that an apparently important effect might have happened by chance alone [and]... we would learn how extremely difficult it is to eliminate subjective bias'.[51]

There are opinions that can in any respect be supported with certain types of evidence, of course, but claims such as there was no holocaust, or Covid is a 'scamdemic' or 'plandemic' is just plainly wrong. You might debate whether it evolved naturally, by accident or if it was indeed planned as some might claim, but questions over its very existence do not need to be given any kind of oxygen.

In our desire to ensure people have freedom of expression, we should not make the mistake of providing anyone the right to freely express anything or that it can be given equal footing just because it might seem fair to do so. This is a fundamental error and to do so is to wash our hands of our responsibility to make people accountable for things they say that might be among the most repugnant claims to make, e.g., American broadcaster Alex Jones, claiming that children murdered in the Sandy Hook School shooting were actors. He can of course say that if he wants but to provide public platforms to assert this diatribe serves no purpose whatsoever but only serves evident-less conspiracy theories, empowers people like him and heaps further pain and misery on the parents that lost loved ones.

I believe we must challenge each other because that is how we learn, how we grow and how we evolve – by not doing so we reinforce ideas and beliefs that may have no reasonable grounds for even existing and by not challenging we do a disservice to people in general.

Yes, you are entitled to an opinion, but equally it is not a guarantee that it is valid, and if it can be proven as lacking in evidence or credibility, the responsibility falls on you to review your opinion and alter it to reflect new learning. Not to do this is to deny what you might rightfully expect of others, irrespective of whether your values and beliefs are upended.

When you converse, discuss, debate, or argue with someone, you do so with a view to persuading or convincing them that your view has more validity than theirs and thus you will naturally expect them to alter their view if you impress upon them that you are right. Therefore, it is your obligation to honour the same commitment if you have been proven wrong and not to 'double down' on your view because it is convenient to do so.

Yes, you have the right to express your opinion, but it does not automatically equate to it being valid.

19. Social media isn't journalism

For every complex problem there is an answer that is clear, simple and wrong.
H. L. Menchen

Social media isn't journalism! I am here to make the proclamation and that we now need to live by this. Okay, enough of the drama, I am of course not here to make such a proclamation – there are many better qualified to do so, and of course, what does it even mean to make such a proclamation.

We live in a world now that even if we wanted to steer clear of social media, we would struggle. It's hard to avoid and has given everyone a voice and an opportunity to express it. Of course, there are any number of countries that keep a tight rein on how people use social media, the kinds of social media they use and even closer inspection of what they express on it.

There is no doubting that in Western society, we have free rein when it comes to social media. The problem with it is not so much access or the freedom to use it but rather, much of what people post is opinion dressed up as journalism.

The beauty of social media is that it has given people a voice, a voice that for many would otherwise be missing, but the manner with which it is now used has led people to assume the label of journalists or reporters.

Part of this belief has been nurtured by the 'Reality World', i.e., 'Reality TV', but as David Mc Rainey explains, 'the recent explosion of reality programming is a great example of the Dunning-Kruger effect. A whole industry of assholes is making a living off of making attractive yet untalented people believe they are actually genius auteurs.'[52]

We see people write blogs or record vlogs and present them as evidence, or chase after people in the street to conduct interviews with various individuals, yet they represent no media outlet but rather a Facebook group. We've seen individuals present reports on online media channels and purport to be representing 'the people' as they pursue an issue without any endorsement from anyone other than a few friends or like-minded individuals.

About a year ago, there were several individuals that started reporting on YouTube about 5G masts being erected in my hometown. They started to report from the masts with devices that apparently recorded radiation readings – there was no way of verifying if these devices were indeed legitimate, and those doing the reporting seemed to have no affiliation to any journalistic body.

Among the videos they recorded was one from a 5G mast in an area that I grew up in where there was a secondary school. They took it upon themselves to actually enter the school and request a meeting with the principal, and then presented him with a document from 'the people' accusing him of Child Abuse because he was overseeing a system that ensured school attendance and by doing so, he was putting them at risk, and by extension, he was responsible for Child Abuse.

To say it was a little out of leftfield for all sorts of reason is putting it mildly, but we see this kind of 'reporting' increasing. Recently I saw a 'reporter' chase after a member of the Dáil Éireann (Irish Parliament) to challenge him about the introduction of some recent Covid regulations.

Now it's not unusual for a member of the press to chase after politicians to get an exclusive or to question them on a breaking story, but first he wasn't a registered journalist, and secondly, the nature and manner with which he was conducting the 'interview' raised many ethical questions, not least of all his approach, which included literally talking into the politician's face.

We have also seen the likes of self-appointed 'journalist' Tommy Robinson be found guilty of among other things stalking, making false accusations and contempt of court as he has 'endeavoured' to appear as the journalist reporting on various news stories, all of which was to try and provide evidence to back up a range of claims.

This growing trend of individuals becoming self-appointed 'journalists' or 'reporters' in an effort to support their claims is at the very least worrying and at best dangerous. Now, this is not to say that we have not observed a history of journalists and reporters, even with their recognised credentials, not being guilty of misleading, lying or exaggerating, but most journalists have come through a process of graduating, plying their trade, are employed by a recognised media outlet, and registered as a journalist.

Whether they are a journalist with integrity is then open to debate but what is clear, that the self-appointed do not represent journalism. All too often we see on social media, the self-appointed 'reporting' and uploading 'stories' to social media, often carefully edited, but conducting their reporting that is designed to make the person they are approaching look as if they are the aggressor or refusing to co-operate.

We also see posts from various campaign groups that have been formed on social media, or personalities, or celebrities, and activists, purporting to represent the interests of many, sharing their opinions which are often ill-informed, exaggerated, or misleading, and this being held up as legitimate reporting or widely shared because it's presented as facts or reality.

I have seen so many friends on Facebook without a moment's hesitation sharing all manner of things without so much as checking the source to see if it has any merit, or if indeed there is any truth in the claims, or if it has any real validity or credibility. And even when it is relatively easy to discredit the claims, those sharing them double down on them and go into rants with all manner of counterclaims and labelling those challenging them as 'sheep' just before the vitriolic outbursts begin, although some just go straight to that first.

People of course can share what they want, that's their right to do so, but I have a right to challenge it – if you put something up on social media, there is no law that says that you can't be challenged. However, the main point in this is that so many posts are presented as stories, reports, or articles from reputable sources, and shared without so much as a checking of the source, where they are coming from (and I don't necessarily mean geographically), their motivation for what they have written or videoed, their connection with the claim, and if the claim hasn't already been fact-checked by reputable outlets such as *Reuters* Either way, just because it's posted on social media does not mean it is journalism.

20. Don't deal with the what should be or what might be – deal with the what is

Life is not about waiting for the storm to pass, it is about learning to dance in the rain.

Unknown

One of the most dangerous words in the English dictionary is I do solemnly declare: *should*! I began to realise its potency back in the mid-90s whilst working at a peace and reconciliation centre in my hometown. I would often hear my then line manager and Director of the centre say 'don't use the s-word'.

On first hearing this (he was talking to someone else at the time), I thought he was referring of course to the word 'shit' and that he had been offended that someone might use such terminology in front of him, which I thought was good to know (in advance) as I wasn't averse to using colourful language myself, let's say.

In overhearing this, I along with the other person that he was talking to at the time (I cannot remember for the life of me who this was), were both delighted to discover for different reasons – relief on his part that he hadn't inadvertently offended my line manager, and from my point of view, I could ignore what I thought was a warning of sorts and that I did indeed have his 'blessing' to use colourful language as I wished.

At the time I didn't realise quite the impact it would have on my thinking in later life, but I can trace it back to that moment – the word is indeed dangerous. It's fairly innocuous, of course, not like fatal, or lethal, or assault, rape or murder, but its potency is not because it is located in the result or outcome of the situations I have just described but rather tends to relate more to people's expectations, e.g., things *should* be this way, he *should* have done that, she *should* have said this, they *should* have said no and so on, you get the picture I suspect.

The word 'should', is overtly anti-pragmatic and works most effectively with hindsight, but of course hindsight never exists in the present. People become bogged down with the detail of what *should* have happened and close out the possibility of learning, because there's an emotional attachment that comes with it – judgement, blame, responsibility, etc.

There is of course a time to look back and reflect and consider what someone *should* have done but in the immediacy of any one particular situation where the desired outcome is not the one that was sought or planned, it's easy to cast aspersions and be self-righteous.

This of course is one of the dangers of the word 'should', as if we could have acted differently, that is, distinguishing ourselves from the guilty parties, as if to say yip, we would be in full control of the outcomes because we are better and we are cleverer than you. Of course, it doesn't always work out like that.

The message that my boss was conveying that day in the office was not so much that he didn't like the word (although it was clear he had a certain distaste for it) but rather, merely focusing on 'should' serves no purpose other than leading to recriminations, judgements, hurt, pain and leaves a legacy where relationships are damaged and it's much more difficult to accomplish what needs to be done.

And so, he was effectively banning the word 'should' and 'forcing' us to alter our language in a bid to find a different approach to dealing with challenges, uncomfortable situations, or outcomes we don't like, need or want (but which invariably bring us the greatest lessons) and ultimately, there's very little we can do about certain things, so let's not dwell on it, let's not deal with the 'what should be' or 'what might be', let's deal with the 'what is' if you know what I mean.

Professor Steve Peters makes an important point about the damage that the word 'should' can do. He describes should as 'typically associated with feelings of failure, blame, guilt, threat and inadequacy... if you had chosen "could" then this would not evolve feelings of failure or set standards. Instead, it is associated with feelings of opportunity, choice, possibility and hype'.[53]

Dealing with the 'what is' is a much better use of energy, and whilst it's arguable that there is a need to deal with what should be done, or should have been done, a focus on the 'what is' provides a more constructive and productive use of time, it takes people away from engaging in emotive discussion in the heat of the moment, and can 'force' people into corners they can't back out of.

Focusing on what needs to be done, i.e., the 'what is' as opposed to the 'what should be' facilitates a process of learning how to manage a situation that demands patience, calm, leadership, conviction, sensitivity, responsibility, and the ability to reassure those that have other expectations, they will have their concerns addressed, will be provided with space and time to be heard, and will have recognition.

This is a fine balancing act because where anyone has a concern, it cannot simply be forgotten, or dismissed, and must be treated with due respect and sensitivity. To focus on the 'should', does not lend itself to creating an environment or climate that is conducive to ensuring stability and continuity.

It does go without saying that where a situation that has arisen is a crisis and requires changing course completely then this is not in question. It would still be a matter dealing with the 'what is' even if it were a crisis but would mean that the need to reflect upon what has happened is not lost.

Dealing with the 'what is' is pragmatic and purposeful and enables obstacles to be carefully navigated. Dealing with the 'what should be' is a process where time and space is carefully navigated and should be underpinned by humility and integrity.

In this lesson thus far, you might have noticed I haven't discussed the 'what might be' yet – I'm not going to – it's a bit of a subset of *should* in any case but can be even worse, i.e., wasting an inordinate amount of time on something that might never happen – the ultimate message in all of this – let's deal with what's in front of us, and make time later to reflect upon what could have been done different.

21. It's not having information that's important; it's what you do with it

Knowing is the absence of alternative or other beliefs.
Daniel Kahneman

Daniel Kahneman's work is known the world over, one of the most respected authors and esteemed writers of his generation, his pioneering work as a psychologist, most notably the books he has penned, *Thinking Fast and Slow* and *Noise* are among the most noteworthy publications of the modern era.

He needs no introduction from me, other than to say if you haven't read *Thinking Fast and Slow*, then make a point of doing so. *Noise* right now is sitting on the arm of one of my sofas alongside a few others – I have this bad habit of reading books simultaneously – wherever I sit there are different books.

Anyways I digress – the title of this lesson seems obvious, but then Daniel's quote seems less so, because surely to know, you need to examine and explore alternatives or other beliefs, right?

Well, yes, of course, but the key message here is that to know something, you need to then separate out what is known from other information and thus what his book *Noise* refers to is what he (and quite a few esteemed writers also) refer to simply as bias. The key point being is that so much of it exists, that we are totally unaware of this, and it unduly influences us. He has proven this in a series of studies and experiments.

In a world of information overload or saturation, it gets harder to distinguish between fact and fiction in amongst all the noise, and so we must get rid of a lot of the noise around us to get the answers we need.

We see this most prominently on social media, where much of the information we need gets drowned out amongst the noise of everyone else posting their opinion, ideas, expertise, theories, and claims.

Trying to make sense of information presented to us in this day and age, is of course quite difficult and as Daniel J. Levitin explains – 'there are three ways we can learn information – we can absorb it implicitly, we can be told it explicitly or we can discover it ourselves, [but the] "onslaught" of "fantastical events" ... [and] being fast-paced doesn't give the chance to assimilate new information'.[54]

Rolf Dobelli makes the point that 'if we could learn to recognise and evade the biggest errors in our thinking – in our private lives or in government – we might experience a leap in prosperity. We need no extra cunning, no new ideas, no unnecessary gadgets, no frantic hyperactivity – all we need is less irrationality'.[55]

Steven D'Souza and Dianna Renner offer a hint of how we might address this when they proclaim 'we do not know what we are capable of until we hear other people's stories'.[56]

In the current era, it would be hard to argue with the notion that not only do we not listen enough, but what is abundantly clear is that we do not make time to hear other people's stories. Making time to do this re-humanises people but whilst we retain distance from others, it's easy to condemn, ridicule, dismiss and belittle.

It's well known that the greater the distance between people the easier it is to slate them. It's much harder to look directly into the eyes of someone and say what you might say if it were online, particularly if it's someone you might know.

These days we can communicate with virtually anyone we choose – even if you are not friends with someone on Facebook, Twitter and Instagram allows you to engage with people that traditionally and historically would be out of reach. We can comment on anything posted by anyone but often without hearing or knowing their story.

When someone makes a comment, they can instantly reach hundreds, thousands, millions of people, even, and the post can snowball and before you know it, you're facing down an avalanche of comments. People have always had opinions, but in the past the opportunity to pass comment and reach said recipient was not possible.

In the modern era we have access to more information at our fingertips than our parents had in their entire lifetime, or certainly parents of my generation, yet having information is the problem – there is simply too much information to consider. The secret is not so much the information itself but rather what you post is ultimately important.

After the killing of George Floyd in 2019, there was much written about BLM (Black Lives Matter) and much of this focused on debating Black Lives Matter-All Lives Matter. I got into much discussion with quite a few people – acquaintances, colleagues, friends and so on. There was a funny moment when an old 'friend' posted something like this – 'I don't care what you think but All Lives Matter and if you don't like it, you can unfriend me.'

I tried to explain the rationale behind BLM, but he chose instead to unfriend me which of course is quite ironic given the fact that he invited anyone to unfriend him if we didn't like what he said.

I have 'lost' a number of relationships as a result of my challenging some posts but that's okay, it is how it is, but in return I had a number of people contact me, people I didn't know, to say that they really appreciated what I had said or rather written.

My point here is not about my thinking I was right and that it was great to be affirmed by them – I still believe I was right and would not regret my comments even with the loss of those relationships, but rather I had random strangers message me (and even in 2021, I experienced the same on other subjects) to thank me not because it backed up their arguments but because of how I laid out the arguments in detail and made time to explain things.

The learning was not so much having the information but rather how I used it, and this gave me the sense that what I was doing had value. We see this all the time with how people create memes to make an important point. You can see this also with the number of quotations I use throughout the book to crystalise the issue, to challenge, to clarify, to deliver a clear message and more besides.

Remember – it's not about the information you have but how you use it.

22. What you hold as a belief will affect the way in which you handle outcomes or respond to them

The way we see the world shapes the way we treat it. If a mountain is a deity, not a pile of ore... if a forest is a sacred grove, not timber; if other species are biological kin, not resources; or if the planet is our mother and not an opportunity – then we will treat each other with greater respect. Thus is the challenge, to look at the world from a different perspective.
David Suzuki

I do firmly believe that what you hold as a belief or set of beliefs will indeed affect the way in which you handle outcomes or respond to situations that arise so in my mind it's better to have realistic expectations or in some cases no expectations at all.

When I was younger, I had very fixed beliefs about a lot of things, often fuelled by an upbringing that looking back I label myself as a right-wing conservative Catholic. Anyone who knows me in the current era might find that somewhat as a surprise but yes, I was, and I was somewhat unrepentant about it – I had God on my side – I even had a picture of Pope John Paul II on the front of my bedroom door, although the real shrine was inside the bedroom door – to Liverpool FC, as my walls were adorned with all things red and white!

At one stage of my life, I took to reading the Bible on a nightly basis. I can't in any way imagine contemplating that now. At one point my favourite book was the Book of Revelations such was the awe in which I held religious scripture.

I held very strong beliefs, and 'argued the bit' on quite a few occasions (I of course had God on my side), particularly with those I hung around with at the time – this is what faith does to you. I'm certain many thought I was a pain in the ass, or full of my own shit or bordering on being painfully arrogant – arguably they were right. Some might still say I am but not because of any religious conviction but that's another conversation.

Like most people, I still have strong convictions about some things, and I still enjoy a good old argument, but these days I tend to try and pick my battles and simply don't subscribe to the theory that having God on my side makes me right, most certainly not anymore!

Essentially when I was younger, I wanted to argue the merits of the beliefs I held to the point that I would hope to 'convert' people. I read a book called *Countdown to Armageddon* by American Evangelist Hal Lindsey and basically was 'hooked'.

He took excerpts from the Bible and interpreted them in a way that made perfect sense to me, and he had credibility so he must be right, and I 'subscribed' as it were. I followed this by reading another book called *The Rapture*, and this only served to reinforce what I already believed.

The power of conviction, style of delivery and 'connecting the dots' all brought me to the point where it must be true. The flip side of this was that I wanted to believe because to believe was to be right, and to be on the right side of God was the way to go, and this mixed with my religious upbringing, and the desire to please and honour my parents, well it's fair to say I was susceptible to having a core set of beliefs.

And as we know, having a core set of beliefs is important, and because most of my peers didn't subscribe to my beliefs, I had to fight for them even more, and I wanted to stand out I guess also, so a perfect storm of sorts, at least in terms of having some sort of identity, which in the teenage years is vitally important, or at least that's how it felt – if only someone said, 'it's okay not to know all the answers, and it's okay not to (already) know who you are', life would have been much easier.

Sometimes you must step back and get some perspective on your beliefs whether that's from family or friends, or studies that have been carried out. Looking back, I can see how much my upbringing influenced me. I'm glad that I have travelled on the journey I have because I can't imagine what I'd be like now trying to respond in this era to many of the challenges faced by those that are religious. Equally, I appreciate that many of devout religious faith draw strength from that as a means of navigating those very challenges.

As we know, people that are religious tend to be more conservative in their beliefs and this often strays beyond their religion into other areas including political beliefs and so when evidence emerges that reflects a wider picture, that's when I allow the evidence to inform my thinking as opposed to hardening my position about existing beliefs.

In his book *I think you'll find it's more complicated than that*, Ben Goldacre, references a review carried out in 2003 that examined 38 studies that contained 20, 000 participants which concluded 'political conservatism was associated with things like death, anxiety, fear of threat and loss, intolerance of uncertainty, a lack of openness to experience, and a need for order, structure and closure'.[57]

We have seen, for example, in the United States, a growth in recent years of Christian Fundamentalism, where much of the liberal thinking that symbolised the US in recent decades is being challenged and findings referred to above are traits that can be found in abundance among conservatives, but more than vocally among Donald Trump supporters.

Many of the views expressed by Trump supporters truly defy logic in many ways, e.g., *Q-Anon*, and are a firm indication that how you view the world is through the prism of your beliefs and this ultimately determines how you respond not only to others but other situations.

This situation is heightened by what Tania Lombrozo describes as 'current trends toward faster, easier, and more seamless information retrieval threaten to exacerbate rather than correct any misplaced confidence in what we truly comprehend.... We have to give up the idea that fast and easy access to information is always better access to information'.[58]

It's further exacerbated by algorithms connecting us to others that share the same or similar views, hence the term *echo chamber*, and this on top of how our brains are designed to see patterns and connect dots and look for information that confirms existing beliefs, then it is becoming more and more difficult for individuals to believe in anything that contrasts with their already established view.

As Dean Burnett points out, 'our brain is so concerned with preserving a sense of identity and peace of mind that it makes us willing to screen anyone and anything that could endanger this.'[59]

If you want to evolve and grow as a human you must be open to the idea of reviewing your beliefs, otherwise you will continue to do what you have been doing and what you hold as a belief will continue to determine how you handle outcomes.

23. Before you condemn, what would you have done?

Don't make someone go through the same thing that ruined you.
Don't hurt people like that.
Unknown

There's an expression I often hear in my part of the world, but it's quite common across both Ireland and Britain, and I'm sure there's equivalent across all languages, and it goes something like this, 'well, it did me no harm'.

This simple expression usually comes from (at least in my experience) middle-aged men in response to their belief that young people these days have it easy (as compared with their upbringing), or can't handle growing up, or are wimps, or now as the term most commonly used, 'snowflakes'. This infers that at the first sign of pressure, or stress, young people melt away, and are unlike those of previous generations who were made of sterner stuff.

In some ways there is a grain of truth in this assertion, just as there is evidence that young people are much more sensitive than previous generations. Greg Lukianoff and Jonathon Haidt's *The Coddling of the American Mind* offers some wonderful insight as to why this is the case, but equally, the notion that all young people are 'snowflakes' is simply an unfair characterisation of a generation of young people that are among the most vocal and committed to creating change that we've seen in a long time.

This accusation of 'snowflake' tends to go hand-in-hand with another broadly sweeping characterisation of young people that they form part of (what is commonly referred to as) 'woke' culture that take offence at everything, and in doing so are on some crusade to get at the older generation, or rather in my experience and observation, the middle-aged generation of white men who are threatened by change.

That supposed change manifests itself in a questioning of existing values and beliefs, and all things convention, custom and tradition. Values and beliefs that they never had much interest, inkling, or capacity to question from their own upbringing or lived experience, so much so that they do not even consider (for one second) if they had any real validity in the first place or whether they might have encroached on others just trying to navigate their way through life. Never mind the idea of their being open to a full-scale review or re-writing of narratives that by and large tended towards a very conservative and black and white way of living.

In the modern era young people are growing up in a time where uncertainty is pervasive, and the guarantees that those now doing the criticising didn't have to live with. They did not have to work in the 'gig economy', house prices weren't through the roof (if you pardon the pun), the cost of living wasn't extortionate, education was accessible and free, and social media and the internet (which is the source of so much negativity and stress) didn't exist.

When I was younger, I got up, went to school, came home, played football and stayed out to muck around with my friends for as long as I possibly could – it really was so much simpler then – aspirations were much less ambitious then, dreams were something that occasionally came true, goals and targets were contextual and relative to the life we led, and the pressure to perform or achieve, was much less emphasised, and competition was something that was largely confined to the pitch or running track. As we know, every generation tends to look back on its own evolution through rose-tinted glasses – it was better, it was easier, we appreciated things more, we were more mannerly, we had respect, we treated people well, and so on. As we have moved steadily into the twenty-first century, it strikes me that the level of criticism targeted at younger generations has reached epidemic proportions.

It has moved beyond simple comparison to one of labelling entire generations – 'cancel culture' for those who challenge convention and tradition, and 'snowflakes' for those who choose to express their feelings and emotions. Further pushback on this often comes in the form of new laws designed to assert and reinforce established 'norms' that ruling parties deem as appropriate, violence against minorities that don't 'fit' mainstream society, and the organisation of groups that are specifically set up to reject and threaten those that do not subscribe to a particular narrative, one that ranges in intensity from conservative and ideological, to fundamental and fascist.

It is oh so simple to condemn others – we do so from a position of distinguishing ourselves from others, to highlight what we would have done differently, how we would have acted – almost always in a more superior way – or that we are indeed superior to begin with in any case. Of course, what separates us from people that will murder, for example, is exactly that ability to distinguish; but I'm not necessarily talking about things like murder, assault, paedophilia, and the like.

We know of many cases, where those we assume to be reasonable and mild-mannered in a Peter Parker kind of way, can be at odds with their normal behaviour, and act in a savage fashion and do unspeakable acts – Germany, Rwanda, and Bosnia, are just examples of where neighbours can turn on one another, even amongst the most passive.

An old friend of mine, or he once was many years ago, was one of the quietest and most softly spoken individuals you could meet. Had you told him the wall was pink (when it wasn't) he wouldn't have argued with you. I met him when I had just turned 16 and we were in the same youth project for about the next 18 months, from approximately 10 a.m. until 4 p.m., Monday to Friday, aside from occasional breaks, when on work placements and similar. I saw him regularly outside of this, went on quite a few residentials with him, and he was in my home on occasion hanging out with me and my family.

The project ended and apart from the odd time I ran into him over the next 12 months, it was less than three years later that he was being arrested for his part in what became known as the *Greysteel Massacre*, a horrendous murderous event in the village I live in. People can change, and dramatically so, this is well known – there's no surprise in that – it happens on a regular basis, and my example is to illustrate this rather vividly.

My wider point is that we condemn people very quickly, but we pay less attention to whether we would behave any differently in the same situation. We of course believe we would and might have good reason to do so, but we choose to ignore the situation people are in and rush to convince ourselves we would act differently. Because of this we should be less inclined to condemn quickly and keener to examine what are the circumstances that someone might find themselves in and why they acted in the way they did. The further we are from something, the less inclined we are to try to understand and the quicker we are to judge. In the future, before casting judgement, take a moment to consider what would you have done.

24. Set some goals for each year – they can be carried forward

Contrary to popular opinion, quitting is for winners. Knowing when to quit, change direction, leave a toxic situation, demand more from life, give up on something that isn't working and move on, is a very important skill that people who win at life seem to have. But don't quit because it's hard. Quit because it sucks.

Unknown

At the start of every year, we hear it and see it – all the New Year resolutions – whether online or in conversations, and as we know only too well, most fall by the wayside within weeks, and even if some are upheld, they often become chores because as we also know, it's one thing to start something, but maintaining it is entirely different. Now, there are of course the few that manage to keep things going and fair play to them!

I make a point of not making any New Year resolutions – I think that by and large they are doomed to failure because the context in which they are made tends to be in an emotional moment caught up in the idea of new this, new that, whilst we are surrounded by others doing the same thing.

There are different points in the year when I think (without much fanfare) yes, I'm going take this on or I'm going to do that, or just simply re-commit myself to thon, but because I don't do it to coincide with any global event, or significant time of year, or in the company of any proclamations from others who want to make their own change, then if I don't succeed, I won't have lost much sleep.

Rather than setting myself up for potential disappointment or feeling a sense of failure if I don't maintain a commitment to the all-singing all-dancing proclamation, I tend to set a few general goals for each year but don't attach a timeline to them, unless of course it is a specific piece of work that is time-bound. I write them on a flipchart and pin it up on a pin-board I have at home.

I write the year inside a circle in the centre of the page and draw lines out from the centre with another circle at the end of each line, and in each circle, I write an aim for that year – there is no start or end date, just something I want to accomplish.

When something is complete, I put a line through it and that's it. If it's done during that year great, but if not, I carry it over to the next year. At the end of each year, I kind of review what's on it and if I want to carry it forward, I do.

The last flipchart I prepared was a bit like the proverbial football season, in this case, 2020–21. I haven't got around to 2021–22 yet never mind even begun thinking about 2022–23, but some of what I wanted to do in the last 18 months has been accomplished anyways. Other things not.

I had another book idea that I was working on but after compiling all the info, and for a variety of reasons, it ground to a halt, and this one took over without it even being identified as a something I had planned, it just sort of happened. I still achieved the overall aim of publishing a fourth book, but not in the year I planned and not with the book I had planned to write. This offers some indication of why dates shouldn't really be set, unless of course as mentioned, it is time-bound and must be completed by a certain point.

Doing things this way tends to create a more harmonious approach to managing expectations as regards the goals I have, i.e., no firm deadlines or start dates and therefore no disappointments and if not achieved by a certain time, I just carry it forward to the next year and next flipchart, of course. It provides a bit of a safeguard in that it not only avoids disappointment but gives flexibility where I need it.

The only real disappointment I would argue is not meeting your own expectations rather than the expectations of others but if you manage them in a way that is conducive to how you achieve your goals then you can accomplish them in a way that is much kinder and cuts you some slack.

The weight of expectation, all too often comes from others without it ever being articulated by others, although sometimes it is, of course. However, we see posts on social media, or we hear commitments from others be it in person, or online, and we choose to 'join the party' only to lose motivation and reinforce often negative perceptions of ourselves when we see others keeping their commitments.

Sometimes, you need to openly articulate your goals to others or at least in the presence of others to give yourself the motivation to achieve them, but this is always tricky in that whilst you feel a sense of obligation to your own perception of what you think others believe about you, it takes away from the more authentic nature of you choosing to set goals for yourself and sticking with them.

We have, of course, moved on from our early hunter-gatherer mode many thousands of years ago when our goals were to find food and try not to be eaten by animals bigger than ourselves – quite motivating when you think about it!

Since then, we have evolved quite a lot where we have had various revolutions – agriculture, industrial, technological – and we also established communities that later became places to live and exchange, which became empires, kingdoms, countries and so on.

We evolved to develop and implement concepts such as work and schooling and set our survival patterns to coincide with the working day and calendar and now we spend our time setting goals to coincide mostly with the expectations of others, our communities, societies at large, and we force ourselves to live in ways that not so long ago were quite alien to our ways of managing day-to-day.

Setting goals has moved beyond a simple pastime to one that has become as much about the power of advertising and marketing, the message of which when you break it down in its most simplest terms is that you are broken, you need to be fixed, you need to have a better and different purpose, and you need to demonstrate your ability to compete with others and earn your right to live on this planet.

Set goals, yes, do it on a yearly basis, yes, but be realistic and give yourself the flexibility needed to accomplish them – don't make things a chore. All goals can be carried over.

25. Learn to write again – it's your handwriting; it's not font or text but yours

If you want to change the world, pick up your pen and write.
Martin Luther

When I die, and (assuming for good reason that) my kids outlive me, it is my intention that I will make the task of clearing out my home relatively easy. I'm always working towards a minimalist approach in terms of possessions and belongings and thus there won't be a whole lot to sort through, mostly books, CDs, and a bit of vinyl, apart, of course, from the usual furniture.

I do try and keep ornaments to a minimum, and at the time of writing I have embarked on a bit of decluttering. It's not that I'm a hoarder, but I do tend to hang on to things and it's only recently I have started that process where you begin to start asking those 'painful' questions – do I really need this, have I used it in the last 10 years or more, and why am I holding on to it?

The last question does connect me to my next point, for example, I have every diary for every year I have worked since leaving school. I have no use for them other than if I need to check back on a date, and that is only with regard to maybe the previous year or so, but I like the idea that when I do pass, my kids can get a sense of what I was doing on a particular date in a particular year.

I have several bookshelves in my living room – not so uncommon I hear you say, and why am I even boasting? Okay, I jest, but on one of the bookshelves, one thing they will find is a lot of notebooks. I've always had a love of writing, and even with all the technological advances there is, I prefer to write by hand (he says whilst typing feverishly on his laptop).

I find (and have always found) writing somewhat therapeutic. I somehow just find the process of putting pen to paper is much more satisfying that tapping on a keyboard – not sure why, it just always has been like that. Perhaps it's down to the time of my growing up – home computers didn't really start making an appearance until I was about 14 or 15, and apart from the normal schoolwork, I was always writing – scripts were one of my favourite pastimes. I always imagined writing plays for the stage – another unfulfilled dream!

And when I was transferring said scripts from handwritten notes to printed format, it was with my old typewriter which I had asked for as my main Christmas present one year – a bit sad really considering computer games were becoming all the rage.

Anyways, I digress. I have quite a few notebooks, of all shapes and sizes and quality, even, clogging up one of my shelves. Most of it relates to projects, or meetings, or events, training, seminars, ideas and so on, and none of it regarding private matters – that will stay firmly implanted in my synapses.

Of course, it is much more efficient to type out things on a laptop – there is no having to transfer scribblings from a notebook and even if you make mistakes, you can quickly delete and type out a new line. But all of this seems a little impersonal to me. Yes, you see the finished products (more or less) on word documents and multitudes of documents can be stored safely on small devices but what documents can't convey is the sense of feeling that comes in a particular moment or what was being imagined in response to what someone else said or the idea that suddenly emerged in a moment of daydreaming.

I know that not everyone likes writing, not everyone appreciates their own handwriting, or even if someone struggles with literacy there's a sense of embarrassment that comes with someone else maybe discovering this after you have passed on and perhaps the idea that someone would discover this is too much to bear (even though you would no longer be around), your worry being that your reputation is somehow tarnished, but pride can still be strong, even after you have departed the scene I guess.

But thoughts, ideas, opinion, scribbles, notes, doodles and so on in your own handwriting belong to you – they are truly what you can call your own and are an excerpt from a moment in time, that might mean much more to someone that was very much part of your life when they see it at a later point, particularly if they weren't aware of whatever those ideas and thoughts were up to then.

Because of the advances in technology, there is a real danger that we might lose the ability to write (not literally of course) but the old-fashioned notion of sitting down with paper and pen. Over the years I have been involved in a lot of training programmes and seminars under Erasmus+ and the one thing that struck me is that more and more participants come to programmes equipped not with pen and paper but laptops, tablets, and phones – it is of course much more convenient and efficient, but there is something much more distinctly personable about seeing someone with pen and paper, or pencil even.

People will of course value the musings you might put in a book, or in an online blog, but just like original sketches by famous artists, or notebooks from famous artists, the value of originals written by hand is what provides the greatest value, whether it is the shape of the writing, the colour of pen, the size of the letters, or the style in which it is written. It is these testimonies to the past created by your hand that will give so much more meaning. It can also be even more interesting to know what had a line put through it, so as to garner in the mind of someone else an impression of what motivated you to change your mind. You don't get that when you're typing on a word document.

When you eventually pass as of course we all will, it's those closest to us, our kids, siblings, friends, and colleagues who want to hold onto and cherish our memories, and to have vestiges of our presence while on earth. My children can, of course, go online and see things I've created, they can read reports I have produced, watch videos of moments captured, and even flick through other books I've written, but having something written by my own fair hand, irrespective of the quality or style, is something that I believe will resonate much more with them.

They can look at the writing, and wonder what was going on in that moment because the style of writing might lean differently from previous writing, the ink might be thicker than other pages of notes, there might be a smooth finish which might relay a message of calm and composure in that moment, or have the appearance of being all over the place, suggesting it being rushed or my having other things on my mind in that moment.

To illustrate more clearly, think about this – which would you prefer, original handwritten notes by one of The Beatles for one of their songs, or a printout of music notes and lyrics? That's what I thought!

26. Create a motto for yourself

Where your fear is, there is your task.
Carl Jung

Mottos – I have more than one so do not hold back – create as many as you want! Mottos or as I sometimes call them, mantras (not entirely sure what's the difference, the latter sounding more like something you say repeatedly whilst the former has the feel of something you say very little but live by), help give me a sense of parameters to work within, as if they guide me in how I manage my life or rather my expectations.

I believe they are important for several reasons – not only guiding you as mentioned above, but to give you a sense of perspective, a sense of control, the ability to manage your expectations, the opportunity to let go of the stresses, to not only hit the re-set button but to set out how things will be moving forward.

They are a chance for you to reflect, to park things, to draw lines in the sand and to decide what you will accept and not accept in the future. They carve out a path that you dig (at least metaphorically speaking), shape, mould and fashion, and where you fill in each layer and in doing so decide what the foundations should be made of.

They give credibility to your beliefs, authority to how you want things to be, authenticity to the things you hold dear, legitimacy to your aspirations and a space to construct meaning.

These are mine, or at least the ones I can remember right now, and I provide an explanation for each. Don't apologise for what you create, but my only note of caution is that they should come from a place of care, self-care primarily, but also from the notion of 'do no harm' to others.

It is what it is – this is for me the great escape clause, it enables you not to get angry, it tailors your expectations and if you adopt this approach for everything, it enables you to better manage your emotions and deal with what is and not what should be (remember my earlier comments on the 'should' word).

Be careful what you wish for – the grass is always greener kind of thing where we eternally seem to be wishing for something more and then we get it, and then realise that the very thing we seek is not quite the attractive proposition we had envisioned and therefore not always getting what we want can be a good thing.

There's always somebody worse off than you – if you are reading this the chances are you have benefited from an education which is a lot more than many people have ever received, and the chances are that it has been free; if you've paid for this book, you've probably spent more on it than millions have to live on per day so just when you think things are bad, remember that there are those less fortunate than yourself.

Humour is the shortest distance between people – I always say that humour is the second last thing that goes – just before your final breath. I fundamentally believe that humour is something we need much more of as it has so many benefits – emotional, physical, psychological, and physiological – there is an immense amount of research that supports this and therefore the need to have more humour in our lives, especially in the current era is beyond any doubt.

It's not a matter of if, only a matter of when – essentially, if I say I'm going to do something, then I will do it, which also is a clear indication of my determination to not make promises I have no intention of keeping, not because I can't keep promises, but as my word is my bond, I don't want to pretend or be dishonest with people about what I am prepared to do.

It doesn't matter what you say, people will talk about you anyway – I learned many years ago that people will talk about you, and they will say what they want to say, even when you might try to convince others of something till you're blue in the face, so whilst it can be exceedingly frustrating, it's important not to give too much energy to someone else's opinion, because in many cases, that is exactly what it is, and unless you have to challenge it, then there are better ways to use up your energy.

Actions speak louder than words – it's an old cliché of sorts but it's true – be defined by what you do rather than the words you speak. I don't mean allowing yourself to be defined by one event, but rather back up your words with actions as over time it becomes fairly apparent if you don't deliver what you said you will do. The only outcome is that people grow to dismiss you, or they lose respect as they will have no faith in your ability to get things done.

Never go to a party you're not invited too – it's more a metaphor but can be of course literal as well, but there will be times when you are excluded, forgotten about and isolated, and sometimes it will be deliberate and other times not so. Knowing the difference or endeavouring to find out in a manner where you keep your integrity will of course be challenging, but there are perhaps reason or reasons for our not being invited, and as much as it is difficult, we sometimes have to contemplate these possibilities and accept them.

You can expend much energy getting angry, hurting inside tremendously or even wallowing in self-pity, but this is not productive and most certainly not healthy. Learning to be okay with invites (any invite) not extended to any of us is hard but trying to understand first is the most important step, and if there is no legitimate reason then you may have a reason to challenge it. Equally, you can also use it as an opportunity to determine whom you should give your energy and time to, and that way you begin to learn whom you need to really prioritise.

As you can see, having at least one motto or mantra can help steer you in the right direction about how you apply yourself in life. Having more than one allows you to determine your actions and behaviour in a variety of situations. Mine of course didn't suddenly appear, they morphed over time, built through experience and learning, but they certainly serve me much better now than in the first half of my life, and this also doesn't mean I can't be flexible, but it does ensure that I use my time and energy much more effectively, and minimises many of the stresses that daily life brings, by determining what things I will allow to stress me, because let's be honest, stress kills and if it doesn't kill you, you will grow older much more quickly.

Make a bit of time, take a pen and some paper, and write down what you want from life or rather, how you want it to be, and how you will live it moving forward, and from this create your little mottos and mantras and begin to practise them. Not only is it immensely liberating, but it is a much healthier way to live.

27. The number of conversations you have is as important as the number of relationships you have

There is no type of affection that can fill the void in a person who doesn't love themselves already. There is no independence in dependency. There is no personal security in attaching yourself to a secure person. Until you have a healthy relationship with yourself, you won't make healthy decisions about someone else.
Unknown

It does of course, go without saying that the need for having friends and colleagues to share conversations with cannot be emphasised enough, but, of course, that's easier said than done. It's not always easy, but even having one person you can share with, or even a few people that might be more acquaintance than dear friend is undeniably beneficial.

The importance of having conversations with strangers can be as important as having someone that you can call upon to talk with. That sense of connection in a particular moment can make a significant difference to your day. For example, you can meet a complete stranger and have the most wonderful conversation yet be endowed with friends but where the conversations can lack substance or any true meaning.

I say this as someone who has lots of acquaintances but only a minimal number of friends, and I must confess that most of those that fall into the friend category tend not to live on 'the island' (as in Ireland). They're spread across Europe and for those that do live on the island, they tend to live in the south of Ireland, so not that close to me (geographically speaking) and by no means that accessible. And therefore, not only are the number of conversations limited, but access to those conversations is limited as well.

Recently I met up with some friends in Berlin following a surprise visit to another friend in Wroclaw, Poland. In fact, both visits were carefully disguised surprise visits to friends along with my son. I prefer to save up money over time and catch up with friends that live abroad rather than having a multitude of regular catch ups at home. For me, there is much greater quality in setting aside more time in a particular moment than regular meetings and visits at home on an on-going basis. My approach is one of sacrifice now for the greater gain. The less numerous, the more memorable as it were.

There are those among us that have lots of friends and/or acquaintances, and mix on a regular basis, and couldn't do without each other. I, on the other hand, don't really have that and if I'm honest, probably do not really look for it either. My friends list has always been much smaller than my acquaintances list, and over the years I have become accustomed to that, and those that were friends in my childhood but were not friends in my adolescence are not friends in adulthood either (except for a handful).

I see this as part of life; people come into your life for short periods, or long periods, and for different reasons move on – part of the circle of life me thinks – and so I am well used to this change. That said, there are quite a few down the years I have got to know, and if we didn't see each other in quite some time, we could easily pick up where we left off.

The important point for me in this, is not that you have a long list of close friends of acquaintances (any kind of list in fact) but rather you know enough people that you can have a conversation with on a regular enough basis, so that the silence that might engulf you and possibly turn to isolation is reduced.

I think there's a pressure on all of us to have a close circle of friends and acquaintances and, of course, whilst this is beneficial, it isn't essential. If you were to scroll through any social media, you might be in danger of thinking that your circle is small or non-existent, if compared to others.

Comparing your own situation with others is dangerous, and unhealthy, because it can simply reinforce any feelings of loneliness or isolation you might experience. Therefore, ensuring that you have enough conversations per week as opposed to having enough close friends and acquaintances to chat with is perhaps a wiser move.

Now, if it turns out that you have a wide circle of friends and acquaintances then great, but either way, work more towards having at least a minimum number of conversations per week, perhaps one a day, one that is significant, and helps you feel that you still matter.

The search for friendship or the company of acquaintances or colleagues can be fraught with difficulties – everything from trying to 'fit in' to knowing how you should behave in certain situations, to being aware of what expectations you should meet. Therefore, perhaps a little more of aiming to having quality conversations as opposed to quality relationships is maybe a more positive way of channelling energies into ensuring that you don't miss out on feeling that you are connected.

Having connection with other human beings is essential, we are, of course, sociable beings. Much evidence has shown that loneliness or isolation is indeed bad for us but the quality of connection, and in turn conversation is much more important. As Wilkinson and Pickett point out, 'it's just not our individual social status that matters for health, the social connections between us matter too'.[60]

Susan Cain points out that even the 'simplest social interaction between two people requires performing an astonishing array of tasks: interpreting what the other person is saying; reading body language and facial expressions; smoothly taking turns talking and listening; responding to what the other person said; assessing whether you'd been understood; how to improve or remove yourself from the situation.... And that's just a one-on-one conversation'.[61]

When you think about it, there is a lot of effort involved. How many times have you come away from an intense conversation feeling quite tired? The importance of conversations cannot be underestimated. David Christian makes the point that 'many components of the good life... include friendship, empathy, kindness and generosity, good conversation, a sense of beauty, a sense of physical well-being and security, a sense of contentment, a sense of intimacy, a sense of humour, and a delight in good ideas'.[62]

You'll note he doesn't say conversation but rather good conversation and therefore it's more about quality than quantity which is something that Sherry Turkle seems to allude to. She argues that, 'Our lives with screens seem to have left us with the need to constantly connect. Instead of being able to use time to think, we think only of filling the time with connection. Why is solitude so important, and why do we want to cultivate it in the young? Solitude is a precondition for creativity, but it is also where we find ourselves so that we can reach out and have the relationships with other people, in which we really appreciate them as other people. So, solitude is a pre-condition for connection.'[63]

Having one good conversation is as important as having many average conversations. The number of conversations you have is as important as the number of relationships you have.

28. Have one weekend away per year where you just leave everything behind

When setting out on a journey, do not seek advice from those who have never left home.
Rumi

Have one weekend away per year where you just leave everything behind – be it with friends or with people you can share time with that you normally wouldn't be in the company of. In my case, it started by accident, well more or less. A colleague (and friend) of mine invited me to his joint birthday celebration weekend (with another colleague) in Budapest, I think it was back in 2006. He and a few others had travelled there the year before (from Berlin, where they live) and it took off from there. They had decided that they wanted to share their thirtieth birthday celebration somewhere other than Berlin.

It was always the last weekend in February – fine for those of us travelling from Ireland – we could catch up on all the Six Nations matches. Over the next 2–3 years, up to 40+ people, all of whom were friends, colleagues, family members and participants drawn from the training courses that my colleagues and I had been organising in and around this time joined us – some for the full (long) weekend, and some for one night only.

Over the years, though, numbers dwindled – people got busy – babies, relationships, marriage, and the novelty of going to Budapest wearing off contributed to only a few of us from my hometown, Derry, in Northern Ireland, keeping the tradition alive.

There was a core among us – namely my friend Matt and I, and occasionally his partner and another friend, Tony, although at the time of writing he has retired from attending – either that or he doesn't like us anymore! Every year some newbies would join us, occasionally returning now and again, but every year it tended to be one or two new people we were able to convince. Also, at the time of writing, we have 'coaxed' two newbies to join us in 2022 – my neighbour, who lived in the same area when I was growing up, and his son also.

Each year we'd arrive late on the Thursday night and visit the famous Ruins Bars, get up late the next day, grab lunch, then go hang out in our favourite Irish Bar, Becketts, and spend the day there before going to the Ruins Bars in the night-time – the same on Saturday and Sunday and home on Monday, sometimes even Tuesday. We were, of course, beat by the end of it… there's only so much drinking, late nights, and different kinds of food that the body can take before it's ready to succumb to exhaustion!

Over the years, we'd meet a core of people that also joined each year or most years – some living in Budapest, some returning for different reasons – a break, to visit relatives and so on. Almost all became like a kind of extended 'family' as it were, all arranging to coincide our weekends at the same time, whether it had been the original intention or not. It sounds a bit silly I know, to leave Ireland to travel to Budapest to spend the daylight hours of that weekend sitting in an Irish Bar – logically and rationally it makes no sense – the point, though, is that it's not really meant to.

The point of it is that for one weekend per year, I'd head off with friends or friend (my son joined 'the family' in 2021) and meet other friends or people we know, and we'd just hang out. No plan, no itinerary, just meet and have some beers, or not as the case may be. If anyone wanted to go off for a break from the frivolity, off they went or they'd go see some sights – there was no obligation to hang out and stay all day, just do your own thing but join us for a while at some point.

And that is the point of this lesson – set aside time with friends, or colleagues, or acquaintances or whatever you want to call them for at least one weekend a year, just to chill, to relax, just to have no plan, just to go with the flow, just to decide to do your own thing when you wish, under no obligation or compulsion to go or be anywhere but ultimately to be disconnected from the grind that is the normal everyday existence.

Of course, this might not be possible if you have kids, or normally work at the weekends, but where you can and people can support you to make it happen, make time to do it. Just to go and not have to concern yourself with the usual stuff is such a liberation, even if it is only delaying things you need to deal with.

It provides a release, allows you to savour the moment, and not feel the stress of being compelled to do this, that or the other. Apart from trying to secure a spot in Becketts so we could watch the Six Nations in relative comfort, our 'itinerary' is one that is epitomised by an easy-going approach. We just simply make time to spend time with each other with no rules – well only one actually – there are no rules, and I don't mean not abiding by laws but rather just going with the flow, having a lot of fun, cracking many jokes, taking nothing too seriously and savouring the time that we set aside for one another.

It really helps to cement relationships, to allow us to spend time with each other without disruption and interruption, and to grow to appreciate each other more and more. It can 'set you up' so to speak for the rest of the year and whilst it's only five days max at any one time, it means so much more because it is short and creates phenomenal memories that act as a motivator to do it again, and again.

It's these kinds of moments where you experience something more than money can ever buy. There are moments when you feel that perhaps you spent a little bit more than you expected to do so on a particular day but then you look around you, you see your friends, colleagues, and family, and you remind yourself, you can't put a value on the costs that you are out in that moment. This of course does not mean you exceed your budget to such an extent that important bills get shelved, but rather, if you can afford to, don't allow the memories to be spoiled by penny-pinching.

Essentially, create memories and experiences that you will look back upon with fondness as compared with the buzz you get from a new 'toy' where after a while the buzz fades. Research has shown in recent times that people are turning more and more towards buying experiences.

In his book *Clarity*, Jamie Smartt reports that, 'Senior executives in the USA were surveyed and asked where and when they tended to get their best ideas. The top three answers were as follows: 1. On vacation 2. In the shower 3. While travelling to and from the office.... Almost everyone can relate to this and find their own examples of fresh, new thought arriving when the mind is in a more relaxed, contemplative state.'[64]

As we say in Derry, 'you'll be dead long enough', so make a point of taking the time once a year – have fun, be silly, tell stupid jokes, be a child again, all in the company of your friend or friends – it really is worth doing!

29. Have one activity per week by which you can let off steam

The greatest of wealth is to live content with little.
Plato

A bit like the previous lesson of one weekend per year, have one activity that you can do at least once per week, maybe even two, three, four times per week and use it to 'let off steam'. In my case, it is football, both indoor and outdoor.

I certainly was not, and still not (as we like to say in our part of the world) any 'great shakes' when it comes to football and especially now that I have entered my sixth decade, although no one could ever say I was lacking in effort, or commitment and energy for the cause. I have developed a reputation over the decades in terms of tackling, but as I like to point out, hard but fair – I have never done any serious damage to anyone yet, apart from myself that is!

Anyways, I digress, what's not important is whether or not I was even that good, or even if I was, it was more about having one thing during the week that I could go and do, and forget about everything else for basically an hour, or a bit longer in the pre-Covid days when we could use the shower facilities at local sports facilities, and continue the discussions, debates, arguments and post-mortems about what happened on the pitch, why it happened and who said what, and so on. Covid put an end to all of that whereas now, like then, you literally turn up for the match and leave again.

Of course, it doesn't have to be football – many have the gym as their thing, or running outdoors, or a walk in the forest, or painting, but what is essential is to have that 'something'. Life is challenging, it can be full of stress, and there must be an outlet of some description that allows you to switch off and just block everything else for a little while.

Again, depending on your individual situation, this is easier said than done, but if you can arrange it, or someone is able to support you then, make a point of it. It really will make a difference to your life, providing some space and time for you just to be able to step out of the daily slog (if indeed that is what your day has become) or at least the daily routine if you need to break up the monotony a little.

I firmly believe that routines need to be broken up, even if it's taking half an hour to go for a walk, or sitting in a different space, or lifting a book and reading a few pages. One of the reasons we get 'stuck' and how it impacts our thinking or lowers our mood is that we don't alter our routines.

We are creatures of habit, and we often continue to do what we have always done and don't break it up. Even the smallest breaks or changes can make a difference because it can remind us that we have the power to change things, and that we have options – it might not always feel like it, but we can exercise choice and small changes, even, can make a difference.

Once we create space and time for even the small things, we can observe how we feel and note the difference it can make and build upon it. That one thing can be something different every week, actually – it's as much (if not more so) about making the time and space to do something that allows us to make a bit of time for ourselves, but at a very basic level it is about taking us out of our normal routine.

I have been playing indoor (and outdoor) football for decades and I have to say, even though it's hard work – the injuries take longer to heal, my stamina has never been great and I'm far from the most talented footballer to ever grace earth, it has been a 'lifesaver' in many ways.

It provides a distraction from the norm, it allows you to 'tune-out' and it creates space for you to be in the moment, to savour the time you have created for yourself. It allows you to let go, to merely focus on what it is you want to do without having to make apologies for it, nor finding reasons to explain or justify it.

With the football, it allows me to keep a little bit of fitness, it allows me to challenge myself to try and keep up with others, many of whom are much younger, not in some kind of trying to prove that I still can kind of way, but rather just to see how I can compete, if I can compete, even it is only to give me a realistic expectation of what I can still manage.

It gives me a sense of realism about what is possible, where I am and how much the body can handle at this stage of life. It's good that it does this – there are many I play alongside depending on what day of the week it is, most of them in and around half my age, and up to a point, you can match them, but only up to a point.

Fitness-wise they're superior, and over so many yards they can steal a yard or two on you relatively easy, and just their ability to turn one way or the other, is always quicker, and whilst it energises me to try and match them, the reality is that they are way ahead. It's not disconcerting though, that's how it is, but it serves a purpose because you come to accept your own imitations and you learn how to be okay with that.

Mostly there's a good camaraderie even in the moments when the red mist descends, but ultimately it allows me to put any struggles and stresses aside for an hour and concentrate on something that doesn't require a lot of thinking or prevents me from over-thinking other 'stuff'.

Whilst many of these benefits relate specifically of course to football, to look at them more broadly is to look at what you are doing – prioritising yourself, making time for yourself, allowing you to be okay with making time for you, pursuing your interest or interests, being unrepentant about pursuing your interests, having the courage to say this is what I want to do and reaffirming that position, blocking out distractions, being among your 'kin' (assuming it involves others), challenging yourself, testing boundaries and limitations, having fun, engaging in meaningful activity, and not feeling guilty about the enjoyment you get from the moment you are in, and wanting to do it again.

So, where at all possible find that something that offers you the space and time to just 'zone out' and if you need to, let off that steam. It really does make a whole lot of difference.

30. Inspiring quotes are important – gather yours

Too many people think the grass is greener somewhere else, but the grass is green where you water it. Remember that!
Unknown

Inspiring Quotes – we all need them, they can help inspire us, or create aspiration(s), or motivate us, or help crystalise in our mind certain things. We all have them and use them in various circumstances and have taken on even greater significance since the advent of social media where they are used ad nauseum to make certain points or deliver certain messages or even pose questions or aid us to reflect on certain things.

Below is a list I have collected or compiled over the last number of years, some of them in-person, whilst others are well known and attributed to a wide variety of individuals, some of whom are famous, and others that are not so famous.

I have made every effort to ensure they are correctly attributed, and some I'm using from sources contained in books by other authors or writers. Some will resonate with you, others not, but there will no doubt be some that have meaning for you and so, without saying much more, here you go, enjoy!

'The meaning and value of art is not trapped in the object.'
Declan McGonigle, Q & A Session on Walled Cities, The Playhouse, Derry, 2013

'All architecture is ideological.'
Declan McGonigle, Q & A Session on Walled Cities, The Playhouse, Derry, 2013

'The victors write the history; the losers write the song.'
Roy Arbuckle, The Playhouse, Derry, 2013

'The best expert you'll ever find in the whole world is your own instincts.'
John C. Parkin, from his book, *F**k It*

'Every day is a blank page that you could fill with the most beautiful drawings.'
John C. Parkin, from his book, *F**k It*

'The corruption of the best is the worst.'
Ziad Hasson, Trans Leadership Conference

'Verbal Expression is the mirror of the mind.'
David McRainey from his book, *You are not so Smart*

'Where we stand, no one else can stand, nor can we stand in someone's place. If we did, his/her place would be crowded and ours empty.'
Amos Davidowitz

'Laughing is about the bubbling up of connection.'
Unknown

'Music is the hotline for our intimacy.'
Professor Nigel Osborne

'An addict is someone who's trying to use a visible solution to solve an invisible problem... the use of drink, drugs, sex, shopping and gambling is an "intervention" that offers temporary relief from their habitual patterns of superstitious thinking, and the painful feelings that often accompany them.'
Unknown

'Each one of us is searching under a streetlight for the key that isn't there.'
Unknown

'Thought is the formless energy that creates the form of our moment-to-moment experience.'
Unknown

'You are not your ideas about yourself. You are not the contents or structure of your thinking. And who you really are is far, far more than you think you are.'
Jamie Smartt, from his book CLARITY

'Clarity, peace and security are only ever one thought away.'
Jamie Smartt, from his book CLARITY

'The Master doesn't try to be powerful although he is truly powerful. The ordinary man keeps reaching for power; thus, he has never enough. The Master does nothing, yet he leaves nothing undone. The ordinary man is always doing things yet many more are left to be done.'
Lao Tse, Philosopher

'When we show up, despite our insecurities, we create new possibilities.'
Unknown

'We have developed speed, but we have shut ourselves in. Machinery that gives abundance has left us in want. Our knowledge has made us cynical, our cleverness hard and unkind. We think too much and feel too little. More than machinery we need humanity. More than cleverness we need kindness.'
Charlie Chaplin, Final Speech from 'The Great Dictator'

'We can always see the mistakes we made but we fail to see the ones looming up.'
Unknown

'You need to help me – you need to let me know when I do things that stop you being who you are.'
Paul Smyth, Youth Work Is Political Seminar, 12 June 2012

'If you don't speak privately, then you can't speak publicly and it's harder to speak publicly.'
Mike Baizerman, Youth Work Is Political Seminar, 12 June 2012

'The future is much too complex to go it alone.'
Steve Lawson, Musician, from a seminar in Poland, 22 May 2013

'Culture is the output of the collective creativity of humanity.'
Ken Robinson

'You have control of what leaves your lips, but you have no control over what is eventually heard.'
Amos Davidowitz

'There are things we can see with our eyes but cannot understand or connect to the realm of our reality.'
Amos Davidowitz

'Once you realise that your clarity, security and well-being isn't dependent on setting or achieving goals then you can relax, and allow your wisdom to guide you... when you are out of habitual thinking you are more closely aligned with reality... your habitual superstitious thinking tends to be about me & my

circumstances – How am I doing? What do I need? How do I look to others, etc?... It turns out that life is less about what happens to you but more about how you relate to it.'
Jamie Smartt, from his book *CLARITY*

'Putting yourself in the right direction means looking forwards to what's creating your experience of life – looking to the source of your thinking rather than the products of your thinking.'
Jamie Smartt, from his book *CLARITY*

'What we have done for ourselves dies with us; what we have done for others and the world remains and is immortal.'
Albert Pike

'Life is hard. Then you die. They throw dirt in your face. Then the worms eat you. Be grateful it happens in that order.'
David Gerrold

'To build may have to be a slow and laborious task for years. To destroy can be the thoughtless act of the day.'
Winston Churchill

'The purpose of our lives is to be happy.'
Dalai Lama

'While we are living in the present, we must celebrate life every day knowing that we are becoming history with every word, every action, every deed.'
Mattie Stepunek

'When you are discontent you look for more; when you are content you look for less.'
Fergal Barr

'You cannot persuade either side to accept the other's view. The best you can hope for is that they get to know the other side's interpretation.'
Amos Davidowitz

'A creative man is motivated by the desire to achieve, not by the desire to beat others.'
Ayn Rand

'If you look into your own heart, and you find nothing wrong there, what is there to worry about? What is the fear?'
Confucius

'Nothing is more dangerous to men than sudden change of fortune.'
Quintilian

'Recognition is the doorway to choice.'
Michael Johnson, BBC TV, 28 May, 2014

'I know how to swing a hammer and I don't need to know the physics of it.'
Allan Cohen

'A promise is not a guarantee, it's a commitment to willingly stand up for it.'
Unknown

'If you don't design your own life plan, chances are you'll fall into someone else's plan. And guess what they have planned for you? Not much!'
Jim Rohn

'Happiness is not a brilliant climax to years of grim struggle and anxiety. It is a long succession of little decisions simply to be happy in the moment.'
Marilyn Monroe

'Our primary purpose in this life is to help others. And if you can't do that, at least don't hurt them.'
Unknown

'My life has no purpose, no direction, no aim, no meaning, and yet I'm happy. I can't figure it out. What I'm doing right.'
Aldous Huxley

'The greatest obstacle to discovery is not ignorance – it is the illusion of knowledge.'
Daniel J. Borstein

'The march of science and technology does not imply growing intellectual complexity in the lives of most people. If often means the opposite.'
Thomas Sowell

'A virtuous, ordinary life, striving for wisdom but never far from folly is achievement enough.'
Montaigne

'We should regret our mistakes and learn from them, but never carry them forward into the future with us.'
Lucy Maud Montgomery

'There are few better remedies for anxiety than thought.'
Epicurus

'It is always wise to look ahead, but difficult to look further than you can see.'
Winston Churchill

'When a man stops dreaming, he stops hoping; but when he learns to dream realistically, he starts living.'
David Wyndham

'No problem can be solved by the same level of consciousness that created it.'
Albert Einstein

'When you are discontent you always want more, more, more. Your desire can never be satisfied. But when you practice contentment, you can say to yourself, "oh yes – I have what I already need."'
Dalai Lama

'Good humour is a tonic for mind and body. It is the best antidote for anxiety and depression. It is a business asset. It attracts and keeps friends. It lightens human burdens. It is the direct route to serenity and contentment.'
Grenville Kleiser

'Too many people spend money they haven't earned to buy things they don't want to impress people they don't like.'
Will Rogers

'Success and failure are emotional physiological experiences. We need to deal with them in a way that is present and calm.'
Chade-Meug Tan

'A life spent making mistakes is not only more honourable but more useful than a life spent doing nothing.'
George Bernard Shaw

'A man must be big enough to admit his mistake, smart enough to profit from them and strong enough to correct them.'
John C. Maxwell

'Be happy with what you have and are, be generous with both, and you won't have to hunt for happiness.'
William E. Gladstone

'Don't wait around for other people to be happy for you. Any happiness you get you've got to make yourself.'
Alice Walker

'If you are not willing to risk the unusual, you will have to settle for the ordinary.'
Jim Rohn

'[The] absurdity of education: its end has not been to make us good and wise.... and it has not taught us to seek virtue and embrace wisdom... we work merely to fill the memory, learning the understanding or right and wrong... wisdom does not require a specialised vocabulary or syntax.'
Montaigne

'Perfection is not attainable, but if we chase perfection, we can catch excellence.'
Vince Lombardi

'Have no fear of perfection. You'll never reach it.'
Salvador Dali

'He is rich who is content with least, for content is the wealth of nature.'
Socrates

'Be careful to leave your sons well instructed rather than rich, for hopes of the instructed are better than the wealth of the ignorant.'
Unknown

'He that is of the opinion money will do everything may well be suspected of doing everything for money.'
Benjamin Franklin

'Most people have no idea of the giant capacity we can immediately command when we focus all of our resources on mastering a single area of our lives.'
Tony Robbins

'Our language has wisely sensed the two sides of being alone. It has created a loneliness to express the pain of being alone. And it has created the word solitude to express the glory of being alone.'
Paul Tillick

'Live each day as if you are going to die tomorrow, learn as if you are going to live forever.'
Mohandas K. Gandhi

'The world will keep turning even if you don't complete such and such today.'
Matt Avery

'People are like dirt. They can either nourish you and help you to grow as a person, or they can stunt your growth and make you wilt and die.'
Plato

'History is not merely what happened: it is what happened in the context of what could have happened.'
Hugh Trevor-Roper

'While a physical law tells us what is, a moral law dictates what ought to be.'
Ferguson, Scottish Philosopher

'How well each does for himself in adapting to his social environment is not the same thing as how satisfactory a social environment they collectively create for themselves.'
Unknown

'The most urgent question to which the physics of society can contribute is whether we can construct a society blessed with the wisdom and compassion that others, often in a harsher or more difficult times were able to glimpse and to demand.'
Phillip Ball

'Laughter is the sun that drives winter from the human face.'
Victor Hugo

'Indeed, it may well be the complexity of modern living in developed countries and the sheer baffling array of commodities, amusements, possessions, opportunities, luxuries, and even what we have to think of as necessities, which causes much of the unhappiness we sometimes feel.'
Matt Avery

'Raise expectations for yourself and the people you love. Lower expectations for the things you cannot control.'
Jamie Smartt, from his book *CLARITY*

'You must fight back your behaviour and learn to fail with pride. Failing is the only way to ever get the things you want out of life.'
Unknown

'Learn to say what you mean, exactly what you mean. If you want people to do something, they need to understand. A main source of conflict between people comes from people not saying what they really mean, and afterwards they get angry because the other did not understand.'
Amos Davidowitz

'An unbiased appreciation of uncertainty is the cornerstone of rationality.'
Epicurus

'Friendship [is] a minor conspiracy against what other people think as reasonable.'
Montaigne

'Fulfilment was to be reached not by avoiding pain but by recognising its role as a natural, inevitable step on the way to achieving good.'
Unknown

'Knowledge is only a rumour until it lives in the muscle.'
Unknown

'I measure the spiritual health of our family by how much dancing is happening in our kitchen.'
Brene Brown

'The only true currency in this bankrupt world is what you share with someone else when you're uncool.'
From the film, *Almost Famous*

'To watch us dance is to hear our hearts speak.'
Hopi Indians

'A nation cannot survive without a sense of national identity and that identity cannot arise without at least some degree of uniformity of culture.'
Unknown

'Value silliness as a wonderful commodity that helps to take ourselves less seriously.'
Lesley Lyle

'People are prepared to sacrifice their personal happiness today in order to invest in potential happiness in the future, and if their plans fail, they can feel as though they have somehow been checked out of happiness they truly deserve.'
Unknown

'Every human interaction is an opportunity to learn even if it's only an opportunity to re-learn or re-affirm what you already know.'
Fergal Barr

31. Identify the things you think (as a society) we need to deal with

Knowing what must be done does away with fear.
Rosa Parks

Did you know that 'Statistically, a black child born in the UK has a 1 in 17 million chance of becoming prime minister, while a white child has a 1 in 1.4 million chance, and a white child with a public school (not state-funded) education and a degree from Oxford University has a 1 in 200, 000 chance.'[65]

Were you aware that '60% of America's rapists, 72% of juvenile murders and 70% of long-term prisoners grew up in fatherless homes?'[66]

Can you believe that 'eight billionaires' control as much wealth as the poorest 50 per cent of the world?'[67]

If I told you that 'today, around 40 million Americans are thought to be suffering from a mental illness?'[68] what would be your reaction?

Pankaj Mishra warns us that the 'two ways in which humankind can self-destruct – civil war on a global scale, or destruction of the natural environment – are rapidly converging'[69] whilst Paul Mason warns us that 'to make the OECD's central growth scenario work, Europe and the USA have to absorb 50 million migrants each between now and 2060, with the rest of the developed world assimilating another 30 million.'[70]

Henry Timms & Jeremy Heimans tell us how 'the fear of automation and the stark realties of income stagnation and rising inequality are all feeding this sense of alienation'[71] whilst Davies and Cape, describe how 'amidst the political reactions against technocrats, there is a more profound philosophical change under way that is altering the role of knowledge and feeling in society'.[72]

Enriquez and Gullans remind us that 'almost every aspect of human life has changed – moving from rural to urban, living in an anti-septic environment, eating very different sugars, fats and preservatives, experiencing novel man-made stimuli, ingesting large quantities of medicines and chemicals, being sedentary; and living outdoors'.[73]

It really is hard to stand back and look at all that is going on around us and not feel ever so slightly over-whelmed. I have spent a while reflecting on issues that affect us and the impact from all of this 'progress' (or at least change) in recent decades that can, I believe, be best described overleaf.

It might appear that I choose to concentrate on the negative as it were, but I suggest it is more a case of identifying the issues that I believe we now face, or rather we should face up to, and adopt a much more pro-active stance towards.

What I write below is for me where I think things are at in this moment in time and reflects what I see are the many pressing issues we need to deal with. I describe the challenges under nine themes and break them down into sub-headings.

These of course are my take on things as they stand and don't necessarily constitute 'the truth' but I would argue for lots of reasons that all are credible and hard to argue against and at the very least we should do more to counter these issues.

---

1. **Degenerative Approach to life and those around us** – Individualism, Competition, Lack of Solidarity, Endless Targets, Growing Distrust, Managed Exploitation, a 'Fix You' Mentality, Imbalanced Lifestyle, Pointless Priorities, Constant Measurements, Misplaced Ambitions, Misogyny and 'the Binary Mindset'

---

2. **Growing Isolation and Disconnect with one another** – disconnection, loneliness and 'safetyism'

3. **Increasing Acceleration and our inability to keep up** – erosion of the 'Four second rule', adaptation and invasiveness

4. **A Pervasive Collective Narcissism** – growth in the 'Attention Economy' and Insecure Narcissism

5. **Increasing levels of Stress** – Fragility, Decreasing Resilience and Pervasive Technology

6. **Addiction to Screens** – 'Screen Time' and 'Magical Promises'

7. **Dilution of our Mental Capacity** – lack of Critical Thinking, Information Overload and Fixed Mindset

8. **Decreasing levels of meaningful engagement with others** – Restricted Childhoods and Modern Disorders

9. **Illusion Vs Reality** – Sexualisation of Young People

1. Degenerative Approach to life and those around us

- **Individualism: the emergence of 'the individual'** – 'the more advanced and industrialised an economy, the more individualistic the culture – and thus the faster the country's speed.'[74]
- **Competition: life is dominated by competition rather than co-operation** – we have been led to believe that we are naturally competitive rather than our true self which through extensive research has revealed that we are actually rather co-operative beings.
- **Lack of Solidarity: the loss of the idea that we should care for, or support people in a way that puts their needs first or at least on an equal footing with ours** – 'our tendency is to stop seeing ourselves as people striving together to overcome our common problems – and to view ourselves instead as people striving against each other to overcome our individual problems.'[75]
- **Endless Targets: we focus much more on results than efforts** – we have been convinced that outcomes are more important than process or experience even though research has shown, particularly in terms of outcomes for young people, that process is more important than results.
- **Growing Distrust: breakdown of trust in traditional institutions, e.g., churches, politics, media, etc** – the result has been a lack of faith in experts and in the era we are now in, we have seen how this is hampering efforts to deal with many of the real challenges all our species face – health and climate change only being two of the most prominent in recent years.
- **Managed Exploitation: viewing humans as a commodity in the shape of data to be manipulated** – 'the more we see the human being as a technology to

be enhanced, the greater the danger of applying this same market ethos to people and extending our utility value at the expense of others.'[76]

- **'Fix You' Mentality: the popularity of alternative medicines and treatments,** e.g., 'back to nature living, various niche organic foods, homeopathies, vitamin therapies, detoxifications, etc., grows year after year, even when scientific studies fail to support them.'[77]

- **Imbalanced Lifestyle: living to work, rather than working to live** – 'we are harder workers, shorter sleepers, and faster thinkers.'[78]

- **Pointless Priorities: expending energy on things that don't meet our expectations** – 'people are prepared to sacrifice their personal happiness today in order to invest in potential happiness in the future.'[79]

- **Constant Measurements: setting ourselves up for disappointments by choosing the wrong measures to judge success by** – 'most people tend to measure their life in terms of success or failures, and their successes and failures in terms of possessions and wealth... [yet] most people rate their relationships with their family and friends as the most important things to them.'[80]

- **Misplaced Ambitions: not every solution has to be technological** – 'the computer power needed to create one bitcoin consumes at least as much electricity as the average American household burns through in two years.'[81]

- **Misogyny: our collective failure to address why we blame women for everything and continue to deny them equality of opportunity** – a 2015 McKinsey Report titled 'The Power of Poverty', found that by closing the gender pay gap and unleashing the full power of women, an additional $12 trillion could be added to the global GSP.

31. Identify the things you think (as a society) we need to deal with

- The 'binary mindset': – the internet does not entertain conversation, discussion, or negotiation... it merely offers an either/or approach where polarisation has grown.

2. Growing Isolation and Disconnect with one another

- Disconnection: we are at our most connected we have ever been, yet we have an epidemic of loneliness – according to the WHO [World Health Organisation], depression has even become the biggest health problem among teens and will be the number one cause of illness worldwide by 2030.[82]
- Loneliness: has led to major health issues – 'loneliness (involuntary isolation)... [it] is strongly associated with depression, paranoia, anxiety, insomnia, fear and health, partly because it enhances production of the stress hormone cortisol, which suppresses the immune system.'[83]
- 'Safetyism': in today's culture intent no longer matters – only perceived impact matters now and very little consideration is given to intention when one person aggrieves another.

3. Increasing Acceleration and our inability to keep up

- 'Four second rule': (drawn from a study in 2006 by Akamai Technologies) where people were prepared to wait for up to four seconds for information to download has now been reduced to a quarter of a second[84] – impatience has become the dominant feature and whereas in the past, people were prepared to wait up to four seconds for info to download this is no longer the case – this is an illustration of where we are prepared to wait much less for things than in days gone by and is reflective of a growing impatience among people in general.

- **Adaptation: technology is moving faster than we can adapt to it** – we do not have (what Rutger Bregman calls) the 'mental bandwidth' to keep pace with it.
- **Invasiveness: Amazon has patented a technology that detects who is speaking at any moment,** and gradually develops a profile of their personality and tastes... this is known as 'voice-sniffing' technology. In her book *Surveillance Capitalism*, Shoshanna Zuboff writes extensively of how there is a growing invasive nature in our everyday lives from technology. She makes the broad point that whilst we can't reverse the gains that technology has made, we do not have to accept all elements of it, particularly those that gather much of our personal information for the purposes of selling it to third parties to exploit us.

4. A Pervasive Collective Narcissism

- **'Attention economy': where everything we put online is designed to get a reaction** – but with it, outrage has seemingly become its most potent currency.
- **Insecure narcissism:** – as opposed to a rise in genuine self-esteem caused by an increase in what has been called 'Social Evaluative Threat'.[85]

5. Increasing levels of Stress

- **Fragility: The 'IGeneration' (those born between 1995 and 2012) suffers from far higher rates of anxiety and depression** than did Millennials at the same age – and higher rates of suicide.[86]

31. Identify the things you think (as a society) we need to deal with

- Decreasing Resilience: The *average student is now more anxious at the end of their study than at the beginning* – by the late 1980s the average American child was more anxious than child psychiatric patients in the 1950s.[87]
- Pervasive Technology: *Twenge* [Jean] *believes that the rapid spread of smartphones and social media into the lives of teenagers, beginning around 2007,* is the main cause of the mental health crisis that began around 2011.[88]

6. Addiction to Screens

- 'Screen Time': Children and young people now spend much more of their lives in front of a screen – studies have shown that more than 2 hours screen time per day can be damaging.[89]
- 'Magical Promises': screens mean kids can always be in control – this raises their level of expectation (about things going their way) but reduces their ability to manage responses that counter this.

7. Dilution of our Mental Capacity.

- Critical thinking: and the ability to source and critique evidence – the general trend has moved away from acquiring deep knowledge... at a time when there is unprecedented capability for finding the explanation.[90]
- Information Overload: we now digest much more information than our parents and grandparents but as Herbert Simpson describes, *a wealth of information creates a poverty of attention*[91] – it's estimated that we create 1.7mb of information per second.[92]

- **Fixed Mindset:** Those unable to contemplate a change in their thinking are locked into a process of proving themselves even against overwhelming evidence.[93]

8. **Decreasing levels of meaningful engagement with others**

- **Restricted childhoods:** – younger Millennials and especially members of iGen (born in and after 1995) have been deprived of unsupervised time for play and exploration.[94][95]
- **Modern disorders: Growth in disorders that reduce the capacity to engage with others effectively:** are markedly anti-social traits: ADD, ADHD, PDD (Pervasive Development Disorder), AS, SID (Sensory Integration Dysfunction) and ASD... studies have shown that students who spend time alone are less likely to be empathetic.[96]

9. **Illusion Vs Reality**

- **Sexualisation of Young People: The 'removal' or perhaps the reduction in the length of adolescence as children and young people jump from childhood into an adult world** – 'In the years between 2009 and 2012, 4562 minors committed 5, 028 sex offences in Britain. The children, some of whom were as young as 5, "mimicked" behaviour seen in porn, often viewed online.... 1/2 of sex offences committed against juveniles in the US are by other children'[97] – we like to think that our children and young people are still innocent and/or naive but the reality is that even at a young age, our children and adolescents are being slowly sexualised.

32. Books (that) will change the way you think!

A child who reads will be an adult who thinks.
Unknown

In June 2013, my (then) full-time job came to an end, or rather funding came to an end. Over the next eight years, I've had full-time work for about one-third of that time, with much of the remainder being freelance, and periods of unemployment. I decided after funding ended to make time to read as it was clear I was going to have more time on my hands. And I did. In the sector where I work, we often complain that we're so busy doing our work, i.e., designing, developing, planning, delivering, monitoring, etc., that we don't have enough time for reflection.

With time on my hands, I made a commitment to educate myself more about why things do happen and understand better the reasons for it. Long story short, I bought lots of books with a view to becoming better informed – some recommended, some I discovered myself whilst exploring good bookshops with a wide selection of non-fiction. The most important thing for me was to make time to read, seek out and find recommendations and share my recommendations with others. So, here it is – the list of books that I have read and suggest checking out.

1. *Age of Anger: A History of the Present*, Pankaj Mishra, Penguin, 2018
2. *Beyond Human Nature, How Culture and Experience Shape the Human Mind*, Jesse J. Prinz, W.W. Norton Company, 2012
3. *Clarity, Clear Mind, Better Performance, Bigger Results*, Jamie Smart, Captsone 2013
4. *Diversify – How to challenge inequality and why we should*, June Sarpong, HQ, 2019

5. *Evolving Ourselves: How Unnatural Selection Is Changing Life on Earth*, Juan Enriquez and Steve Gullans, Oneworld Publications, 2015
6. *Flipnosis, The Art of Split Second Persuasion*, Kevin Dutton, arrow books, 2011
7. *Freakonomics: A Rogue Economist Explores the Hidden Side of Everything*, Steven D. Levitt & Stephen J. Dubner, Penguin, 2015
8. *F**k It, The ultimate spiritual way*, John C. Parkin, Hay House, 2011
9. *I think You'll find it's more complicated than that*, Ben Goldacre, Fourth Estate, 2015
10. *Know This: Today's Most Interesting and Important Scientific Ideas, Discoveries and Developments*, John Brockman, Harper Perennial, 2017
11. *Laugh Your Way to Happiness: Using the Science of Laughter for Total Well Being*, Lesley Lyle, Watkins Publishing Limited, 2014
12. *More Human: Designing a World Where People Come First*, Steve Hilton, W H Allen, 2015
13. *Nervous States: How Feeling Took Over the World*, William Davies, Jonathan Cape, 2018
14. *Not Knowing: The Art of Turning Uncertainty into Opportunity*, Steven D'Souza, Dianna Renner, LID Publishing Ltd, 2016
15. *Out of the Wreckage: A New Politics for an Age of Crisis*, George Monbiot, Verso, 2017
16. *Cultivating Peace: Becoming a 21st-Century Peace Ambassador*, James O'Dea, Shift Books, 2012
17. *Quiet, The Power of Introverts in a World That Can't Stop Talking*, Susan Cain, Penguin Books, 2013
18. *Rethink: The Surprising History of New Ideas*, Steven Poole, Scribner, 2016
19. *Secrets of Happy People*, Matt Avery, Teach Yourself, 2014

20. *Stuffocation: Living More with Less,* James Wallman, Penguin Books, 2015
21. *Team Human,* Douglas Rushkoff, W.W. Norton & Company, 2019
22. *The Art of Thinking Clearly,* Rolf Dobelli, Sceptre, 2013
23. *The Chimp Paradox: The Mind Management Progrmme for Confidence, Success and Happiness,* Prof Steve Peters, Vermillion London, 2012
24. *The Coddling of the American Mind,* Greg Lukianoff and Jonathon Haidt, Allen Lane, 2018
25. *The Compassionate Mind,* Paul Gilbert, Constable, 2013
26. *The Great Acceleration, How the World Is Getting Faster,* Robert Colville, Bloomsbury Publishing, 2016
27. *The Growth Delusion: The Wealth and Well-Being of Nations,* David Pilling, Bloomsbury Publishing, 2019
28. *The Idiot Brain: A Neuroscientist Explains What Your Head Is Really Up To,* Dean Burnett, Guardian Books, 2016
29. *The Organised Mind: Thinking Straight in the Age of Information Overload,* Daniel J. Levitin, Viking 2014
30. *The Phoenix Generation: A New Era of Connection, Compassion, and Connectedness,* Kingsley L. Dennis, Watkins Publishing, 2014
31. *The Road Less Travelled: A New Psychology of Love, Traditional Values & Spiritual Growth,* M. Scott Peck, arrow books, 2006
32. *The Rules of Life: A Personal Code for living a better, happier, more successful kind of life,* Richard Templar, Pearson, 2012
33. *The Spirit Level: Why Equality Is Better for Everyone,* Richard Wilkinson and Kate Pickett, Penguin Books, 2010
34. *The Stupidity Paradox: The Power and Pitfalls of Functional Stupidity at Work,* Mats Alvesson & Andre Spicer, Profile Books, 2016
35. *This will make you smarter: New Scientific Concepts to Improve Your Thinking,* John Brockman, Transworld Publishers, 2012

36. *Thinking Fast and Slow*, Daniel Kahneman, Penguin Books, 2011
37. *Utopia for Realists and How We Got There*, Rutger Bregman, Bloomsbury, 2018
38. *What should we be worried about? Real Scenarios That Keep Scientists Up at Night*, John Brockman, Harper Perennial, 2014
39. *We are our brains:, From the Womb to Alzheimer's*, Dick Swaab, Penguins Books, 2014
40. *Who can you trust? How Technology Brought Us Together and Why It Could Drive Us Apart*, Rachel Botsman, Penguin Business, 2018
41. *You Are Not So Smart, Why Your Memory Is Mostly Fiction, Why You Have Too Many Friends on Facebook and 46 Other Ways You are Deluding Yourself*, David Mc Rainey, One World, 2012
42. *Why Women are blamed for everything: Exposing the Culture of Victim Blaming*, Dr Jessica Taylor, Constable, 2020
43. *The Web of Meaning*, Jeremy Lent, Profile Books, 2021
44. *The Lonely Century: Coming Together in a World that's Pulling Apart*, Noreena Hertz, Sceptre, 2020
45. *The Tyranny of Merit: What's Become of the Common Cause*, Michael J Sandel, Allen Lane, 2020
46. *Humankind: A Hopeful History*, Rutger Bregman, Bloomsbury Publishing, 2020
47. *The School of Life: An Emotional Education*, Hamish Hamilton, 2019
48. *The Precipice: Existential Risk and the Future of Humanity*, Toby Ord, Bloomsbury Publishing, 2020
49. *Rebel Ideas: The Power of Diverse Thinking*, Matthew Syed, John Murray Publishers, 2019
50. *Creating Freedom, Power, Control and the fight for our future*, Raoul Martinez, Canongate, 2017

33. Understand why things are the way they are and why it has happened

Smart people learn from everything and everyone, average people from their experience, stupid people already have the answers.
Socrates

The last half century (and perhaps more particularly the last 10–20 years) has witnessed a vast increase in the speed and evolution of almost everything, which has resulted in what could be described as an ever-changing landscape – a bit of an understatement if ever there was one!

Let's take a moment to consider just some of the most recent developments.

- between 1950 & 2000, global population increased 2.5 times; food production has tripled
- globally, obesity almost doubled between 1980 and 2014
- the rise in obesity in recent decades also mirrors the fall in sleep duration and quality
- the share of wealth controlled by the top 0.1% grew from 7% in the 1970s to 22% in 2012, and now the same 0.1% own as much wealth as the bottom 90%.
- three-quarters of all border walls and fences were erected after the year 2000
- as of 2008, humanity was consuming 30% more per year than the planet sustainably produces
- there are 28 cities with a population of more than 10 million people; by 2030, the UN predicts that there will be 41 – and more than half will be in Asia
- in 1961 human demand accounted for 0.7 planet's worth of biocapacity. In 2008, it was estimated by GFN

[Global Footprint Network], that we need 1.5 planets to
sustain us.

- it's estimated that there are less than 60 harvests left as the
Earth's topsoil has been slowly eroded due to industrial
farming

We are now in an era, often referred to as the Anthropocene,
where we are no longer shaped by our planet, but where we are
shaping the planet. Creativity, imagination, innovation, and the
entrepreneurial spirit has brought us to this point

Enriquez and Gullans tell us that 'the rapid pace of today's
human-driven evolution may not be giving humanity time to
adapt and to reach a steady state within a new environment'.[98]
Robert Colville echoes this claim when he tells us that, 'the
more advanced and industrialised the economy, and the more
individualistic the culture, the faster the country's speed.'[99]

Roger Schank expresses concern that 'since no one thinks
that they need to think, the news has become a mouthpiece for
views that can be easily parroted by their listeners. Challenging
beliefs is not part of the function of the news anymore.... I'm
worried that people can't think, can't reason from evidence, and
don't even know what would constitute evidence'.[100]

Peter Schwartz describes how 'we are now living in a world
of perpetual crisis and the high anxiety it produces. Crises
are not new... [but] the interconnection of the world's many
systems often lead one crisis to cascade into the next like falling
dominoes... living in a world of high anxiety often leads us to
do the wrong things. We adopt short-term and local solutions
rather than taking a systemic and long-term view'.[101]

Gigevenzer argues that 'the answer to modern crises is
not simply more laws, more bureaucracy, or money, but, first
and foremost more citizens who are risk-literate. This can be
achieved by cultivating statistical thinking'.[102]

To be honest it's hard to make sense of many of the things that's going on in the world, and perhaps, the solution is to lock yourself away at home with a few books, and not look at social media or television for a few days, or even a few weeks, and just do a bit of chilling.

Over the years I have tried to understand what is going on in the world and why things happen as they do. It's clear that everyone understands things in their own unique way, but below is my interpretation of the lessons from the last half century:

- failure of trickle-down economics and a growing inequality
- emergence of developing economies trying to catch up with West
- junk food, obesity, food additives and toxic pollutants
- climate change
- increased levels of stress, anxiety and suicide countered by the emergence of the self-help industry
- endless consumption
- the loss of free play and unsupervised risk-taking
- changes in parenting practices
- changes in the make-up of the traditional family
- re-emergence of East versus West divide
- the dilution of existing democratic states versus growth in authoritarian states
- increasing civil and political strife across numerous countries
- growing political polarization
- growing division between liberal and conservative, urban, and rural, college-educated, and non-college-educated
- increase in the number of border walls
- increased immigration and fleeing of refugees

- growing levels of protectionism
- corruption and the loss of trust in traditional institutions
- increasing campaigns for justice and social justice, as contrasted with social justice versus dilution of human rights
- greater visibility of minorities viz a viz persecution of minorities
- increase in the number of democratic states versus dilution of the rights of citizens in established democratic states
- renewed emergence of nationalism and populist politics
- terrorism and new forms of extremism
- battle for the hearts and minds of academia
- exploration of outer space
- mapping of the human genome
- genetic manipulation and cloning
- growth in geo-politics
- pervasive technology: 'artificial' intelligence, robotics, drones, e-books, audio books, digital books, virtual libraries, blogs, vlogs, microblogs, podcasts, videocasts, file–sharing, video-sharing, social networks, forums, MOOCs, online courses, virtual classrooms, and even virtual universities.

Let's try and understand a little bit more what the lessons are so we can better understand why they have happened, so we can better understand how we tackle them.

34. If you don't know, you don't know

Opinion is really the lowest form of human knowledge. It requires no accountability, no understanding. The highest form of knowledge is Empathy, for it requires us to suspend our Egos and live in another's world.
Bill Bullard

Understanding what's going on in any situation gives a sense of belonging, or more accurately a stake in the situation we are in or the conversation we are part of. It also gives us security and lessens the feeling of threat of exclusion we might get from our not being able to exert any influence or contribute to any outcome that might result.

Huh? What's that I hear you say? What am I talking about? Well in its simplest form, in order to be part of a conversation, or at least to feel part of it, it's important that you can contribute to it, or you essentially lose interest, switch off, and (possibly) before you know it, decisions are made affecting you, that you might not even recall, let along hearing.

Ironically, though, not being fully emerged in a conversation, (even if you do know the subject matter) can be quite liberating – assuming of course that you are okay with uncertainty or having little or no idea of what's going on. It might well be a case of a 'bigger subject' that holds no real meaning for you, such as the Olympics, an election, a freak weather event, the building of an airport, etc.

As Rudy Rucker describes, 'You get a sense of psychic expansion if you begin thinking in terms of an infinite universe. A feeling of freedom, and perhaps a feeling that whatever we do here does not, ultimately, matter that much. You'd do best to take this in a "Relax!" kind of way, rather than in an "It's pointless" kind of way.'[103]

These are perhaps events that you are indifferent too and therefore it's not essential you know what's going on and thus, are pretty laid back about it. However, being laid back about events 'closer to home' might be a little trickier.

The challenge to us all in this situation is being okay with not knowing. Not knowing in many respects is okay. I'm not necessarily talking about what I would call some of the fundamentals in life, e.g., knowing how to cook (within reason), knowing how to wash clothes, knowing how to have meaningful conversations, knowing how to write and so on. I'm talking more so about not knowing what's going on in current affairs, which movies have just been released, who's dating who, what is the latest model of sports car just released, etc.

It is of course nice to be up to date on the latest events, gossip, releases, publications and more, but it's not essential. I have found a certain kind of bliss in not knowing or not trying to keep up to date on what's happening 'out there'. There is an expression that has made its way into common parlance in recent times – FOMO (Fear Of Missing Out). And for many, not knowing what's going on or not being part of something are symptoms of this.

Many years ago, when I was starting out in my Youth Work career, I had the benefit of working in Youth Information, and if someone came into us looking for a query to be answered we would endeavour to find out, exercising all options in the process. Our promise was that if we didn't know, we would find out the answer, and we were committed to finding out within 24 hours. If it took longer, we would still commit to getting an answer.

This of course was 'back in the day' when finding answers was a combination of existing knowledge, textbooks, and other forms of literature, making telephone calls, and a very limited but an early forerunner of the internet, in this case Prestel, the UK's very own interactive 'videotex system' that was launched in the late '70s and was accessible through dial-up. It had a catalogue and so you flicked through the pages to find the subject and then sub-headings. The beauty of this process was the process itself – you kept searching till you came upon the answer.

We did, however, have to accept the possibility that we didn't know things, even though we had all this info at our fingertips, and of course many years before the internet but in accepting we didn't know never resulted in a loss of face, but rather resulted in a determination to find out, and thus we were not going to be defeated as it were. In fact, patience was the name of the game. If your first efforts didn't turn anything up, you kept going.

Becoming accustomed to saying we didn't know was an acceptance that we were also human, that we couldn't possibly know everything, that we couldn't bullshit our way through things because people were depending on us and (sometimes) standing next to you as you looked for the answers.

We realised very quickly that it was okay not to know, and this was at a stage in my life when I thought I knew a lot. It was also at a time when I thought I was right a lot of the time, be that in discussions or arguments, and so had to reconcile this in-built belief or sense that I knew (no idea where it came from ultimately) with the idea that I need to find out, at least to preserve my reputation.

Being able to say I don't know (and inside knowing that it is okay to do so) but working to find out the answer(s) was for me a rewarding process. On one hand I get to change my approach and remain self-assured whilst on the other hand still make the effort to help someone.

As I have gotten older, and apparently wiser, and I now know a lot more, I also realise I know much less; that the level of information 'out there' is so immense that it is not possible, not even conceivable that I'd know a zillionth of all knowledge and thus I have become incredibly content with that. That of course does not mean that I am not determined to keep learning, but I am very okay with not knowing.

If asked to offer some thoughts on a subject I have yet to really explore, I'm honest enough these days to know when to say that I don't know, and that is quite liberating! Not feeling compelled or obliged to have to pretend I know or trying to sound like I know something about a particular subject is quite rewarding.

You become more relaxed, you develop a greater sense of humility, you don't try to dominate, you don't become absolute in your thinking, you don't box yourself into a corner and you don't make claims that you can't really back up.

In an era when we have more information than we could possibly imagine, not to mention greater access to it, this can be to our detriment, of course.

Just as Douglas Rushkoff puts it, 'we now know, beyond any doubt, that we are dumber when we are using smartphones and social media. We understand and retain less information, comprehend with less depth, and make decisions more impulsively than we do otherwise. This untethered mental state, in turn, makes us less capable of distinguishing the real from fake, the compassionate from the cruel, and even the human from the nonhuman.'[104]

If you don't know, you don't know – be okay with that. Being honest about your limitations brings no shame – appearing to try and know stuff only cultivates a certain perception about you among others and nurtures a reputation you're better without. People will admire humility much more than bravado!

35. Develop an ideological statement to help steer your approach to life

Don't be afraid your life will end; be afraid it will never begin.
Grace Hansen

Not everyone will be familiar with the phrase Ideological Statement so let me give it some context. In 1993 I went to study at (what was then called) University of Ulster – some years later it changed its name to Ulster University – I'm sure somebody, somewhere made money from this, but anyways!

I studied Community Youth Work and one of the modules was (if I remember correctly) Community Development. The lecturer who for the first year of my course was also my Personal Tutor (think that's what it was called) until our relationship went 'south', was quite a good lecturer and I enjoyed his classes. I won't discuss my thoughts on his ability as a Personal Tutor – another matter entirely!

We looked at various systems of political thought and ideology that had governed community development during the '60s, '70s and '80s in Northern Ireland, and one way of doing this was for the Lecturer to share various statements from different individuals and challenge us to work out as to what their politics was – liberal, conservative, and socialist among others to give you a sense of what I am getting at.

This task was very useful in that it was the first time in my career I was to consider how I approached youth work. Whilst my relationship with the lecturer cum tutor was strained to say the least, I do believe in giving credit where credit's due, and this was a pivotal moment in my studies and in informing my approach to youth work.

It was the moment that I was asked to make time to consider things like my values, my beliefs, and the politics that underpinned or governed my approach. I was keen to get it right and took time to make sure I did, and I found the process of reflection very beneficial to my putting on paper for the first time how I worked, or rather how I went about my work.

Whilst the statement itself has had some minor nips and tucks over the years, it has largely remained constant, and whilst it's geared specifically towards my youth work career, it has also informed my approach to life more generally. And it's with this in mind, that I have learned the importance of having an 'Ideological Statement'.

Most people have a range of ideologies which they subscribe to, but chances are that they rarely ever write these down, or even try to come up with one overarching ideology. The process of sitting down, putting pen to paper, or finger to keypad, and working out what your values and beliefs are, or where they are located, how they influence you, what you want to achieve with them, what difference you want to make, how you want to engage with or influence people and things, etc., is most probably a rarity.

It's a very useful exercise and gives you a sense of direction and purpose and allows you to make decisions about what you accept and don't accept, what you expect or not, and how you will be with all those other humans that surround you.

Try it, it could be a turning point. To offer some inspiration, or even just to give you a sense of how it might look, overleaf is my statement which is heading towards its thirtieth birthday (at the time of writing).

It is my strongly held belief that the development of individuals should be foremost in our work. It is our inescapable responsibility to share in the development of individuals by at least providing at the outset, the means by which to do so in accordance with their needs and desires.

I aim to provide various settings and environments that will facilitate the journey from dependence through independence to self-sufficiency enabling individuals to establish and assert their individuality whilst undertaking to take account of the environment that surrounds them.

Whilst learning from their experiences it is my hope that they will grow in knowledge and understanding of the processes that have assisted their development.

My intention is to facilitate a process whereby my input supports and creates opportunities for young people to make informed decisions without feeling that they should subscribe to any particular set of beliefs or opinions.

I would hope that I am in fact helping to lay the foundations for each individual to discover their own potential through co-operation with one other and by maintaining a level of dignity and respect in their everyday interaction with those around them whilst striving to achieve an enhanced level of self-fulfilment and expectation.

By helping each young person develop enhanced levels of expectation I am asking them to take ownership of their learning and development so as to create greater awareness of their skills and capacity for learning. By doing so I hope to encourage them to find their own way in life and make the most of their own resources and talents.

It's as important as it is essential that young people should be able to get along with others and be compassionate and concerned about people's needs as well as their own. There is no one setting or method which achieves this but rather a combination, however, young people need to be free to 'run their own show', being encouraged to become involved and given opportunities to develop the necessary skills and leadership to do so.

Overall, I engage in and attempt to facilitate a process of learning based on interaction that helps to create a pro-active environment for progressive change.

The process for me is more important than the actual results but a belief in setting targets provides the springboard to achieve.

I am prepared to take risks to give substance and foundation to the belief that process is priority. I endeavour to employ this approach in my practice at all times.

My commitment to this approach is underpinned by a strong belief in having fun, learning by doing, using humour and being honest.

36. Believe in the power of humour to transform things, people, and situations

Never trust a man who, when left alone in a room with a tea cosy, doesn't try it on.
Billy Connolly

'Humor is a whole mind-body and social experience; it's a cognitive ability that gets our emotions and our bodies involved in the act, and it also connects us to other people.'[105]

It's clear – we need more humour in our lives. This is no false claim. In this lesson, I set out to explain why this is the case. I outline the rationale behind the argument that we need more humour in our lives in order to improve our health and in doing so contribute to the well-being of the nation (replace nation with country/region/jurisdiction/city/town/village/household/bathroom of your choice).

Peter Berger tells us that, 'Humour – that is, the capacity to perceive something as being funny – is universal; there has been no human culture without it. It can be regarded as a necessary constituent of humanity.'[106] Before exploring humour in-depth, let's start with a little journey through time.

Humour – a little history
Humour has a long history, of course, in Athenian Democracy, the opinion of voters was influenced by political satire performed by the comic poets at the theatres – they would portray persons or institutions as ridiculous or corrupt. Can you imagine? Corrupt institutions, in Greece too – of all places, the home of democracy!

Aristotle defined comedy as 'one of the original four genres of literature' which also included tragedy, epic poetry, and lyric poetry whilst Epicurus set up a 'philosophical establishment to promote happiness'. Humour is also referenced in the Bible, 'A cheerful heart does good medicine, but a broken spirit makes you sick' can be found in the Book of Proverbs (17.22). Broken Spirit? Is that a Ghost who lacks a bit of backbone? Sorry, couldn't resist.

> In the late 5th-century BC Greece, a secular school known as the Hippocratic writers made a bid to monopolise the profession [medicine], at the expense of rivals who were attached to temples. They had an entirely erroneous theory of how disease works – they thought that health was essentially a balance between four 'humours'... adjust the balance and you alter the patient's state of health.[107]

Or so the theory went! What's notable is not that the Hippocratic writers were wrong in this case but the weight they attached to the idea of humours – not in the sense we might know it to be now but as means of balance to restore health. That concept or idea is not too far removed from humour, i.e., laughter, happiness, etc., is indeed good for the health – physical, mental, emotional, or otherwise and I will go on to show how.

Anyway, moving on, during the Middle Ages, the term 'comedy' became synonymous with satire, and later humour in general, after Aristotle's Poetics was translated into Arabic in the medieval Islamic world. Early Native Americans had clowns who worked with Witch Doctors – they realised the powerful effects of humour and laughter in healing – the third most important person in the tribe was the clown.

In the fourteenth century, French surgeon Henri de Mondeville used humour therapy to aid recovery from surgery whilst from the sixteenth to eighteenth centuries there are accounts of humour being used for health purposes to address depression, release tension, and restore equilibrium which were related to the concept of the 'four humours'.

Accounts of this are attributed to the likes of Robert Buton (English Parson), Martin Luther (Pastor), Herbert Spence (Sociologist), Immanuel Kant, (German philosopher) and William Beattie (English physician). Don't worry, I had to go look them up too!

From medieval times until the seventeenth century, licensed fools, or jesters (imagine, you had to get a licence to be a fool in the seventeenth century, now we're surrounded by them, see what happens when you don't licence things – everybody's at it) were commonly kept at court and were frequently at the disposal of wealthy nobles – their job was to entertain.

Both the Jester or Clown dates from the fifteenth and sixteenth centuries right up to the twentieth century (and in recent times) made famous by the likes of Charlie Chaplin, Harold Lloyd, Harpo Marx, Marcel Marceau, *The Goon Show* and Mr Bean among many. If you're over 50 (and from certain parts of the world) I bet you can't read Harold Lloyd without signing to yourself, 'Welcome to Harold Lloyd, doo doo doo doo, doo doo doo, Harold Lloyd,...'

In the 1930s clowns were brought into the U.S. hospitals to cheer up children hospitalised with polio. In 1972 U.S. Doctor Hunter 'Patch' Adams founded The Gesundheit Institute (no I swear it wasn't named after a sneeze) – a home-based free hospital to bring fun, friendship, and the joy of service back into health care – but prior to this and perhaps with even more significance, Dr Norman Cousins who was diagnosed with Ankylosing Spondylitis (Arthritis to you and me) in 1964.

He was so depressed by his stay in hospital that he checked himself out of the hospital, hired a nurse and moved into a hotel – yup, clearly Dr Cousins had more money than you and I which begs the question why he didn't do that in the first place – obviously he just wanted to sponge off the system! Okay, only kidding because what he did next was very important, listen very carefully, I will say this only once (in a French accent). If you have seen the sitcom *Allo Allo* you'll know what I did there!

Along with mega doses of vitamin C, he watched comedy movies; '10 minutes of genuine belly laughter had an anaesthetic effect and would give me at least 2 hours of pain-free sleep.' He cured himself of his illness and lived to tell the tale and in 1979 he published a book telling the story, *Anatomy of an Illness*. Yip, No sh** it's true. Even though I'm passionate about humour, finding these things out was a bit of a revelation for me also.

Research into the benefits of Humour

Research has shown that humour has many health benefits. It increases oxygen intake and blood circulation thus lowering your blood pressure; it reduces water vapor and carbon dioxide in the lungs, decreases the risk of pulmonary infection; improves the function of blood vessels and increases blood flow, which can help protect you against a heart attack and other cardiovascular problems;[108] it works your stomach muscles, boosts your immune system, releases natural painkillers in the body, reduces stress levels, boosts the body's production of infection-fighting antibodies and helps your body recharge. Bet you're feeling better already. And if you haven't had a heart attack yet then this proves the point! In a nutshell, humour achieves the following:

Physical Health Benefits	Mental Health Benefits	Social Benefits
- Boosts immunity - Lowers stress hormones - Decreases pain - Relaxes your muscles - Prevents heart disease	- Adds joy and zest to life - Eases anxiety and fear - Relieves stress - Improves mood - Enhances resilience	- Strengthens relationships - Attracts others to us - Enhances teamwork - Helps defuse conflict - Promotes group bonding

There is clearly 'mountains' of evidence of the benefits of laughter yet the problem these days, at least from my perspective is that we don't laugh enough and when we do it seems to be temporary, a form of escapism or at the expense of others (and I'm not talking about the banter you share with your friends where it is a little bit of fun and you know it's not to be taken seriously, in fact, it's merely a term of endearment with your friends) where you use humour in a negative fashion to dismiss, diminish, or belittle people.

Along with a number of colleagues, I have been involved in the delivery of a training programme called *Humour Is Serious Business* where we try to promote a way of thinking, a state of mind which encourages people to see humour in all things – this doesn't mean neglecting obligations and responsibilities nor making light of important matters but changing perspective but 'to find things funny we need to be able to shift perspective, perceive incongruities and paradoxes, and be surprised and delighted by the unexpected – the punch line. This causes us to switch into a playful, rather than a serious, frame of mind. When we are amused, we are in a state of observation, which gives us a bit of psychological space or distance from our circumstances'.[109]

Dr Suzanne Phillips writes,

As humans we are one of a few species that laughs and our laughter spans age, gender, language and culture. Laughter is not just a by-product of happiness. Given the body-mind connection, the very act of laughter changes body chemistry to our advantage.... Research finds that laughter can improve diseases like asthma, cancer and heart disease by reducing the physiological stress response that exacerbates these conditions.[110]

Okay, time for the more serious stuff... ironically...

The irony of the age we now live in is that whilst we have had so many advances in science, technology, medicine, and health care, we live in an age where instances of stress alongside more serious issues such as depression and suicide have much greater prominence.

over the last half-century, we have grown used to the idea that we live to work, work to earn, and earn to consume. We consume not just to survive and flourish and enjoy our lives, but to signal who we are and where we stand in the world, especially in relation to others. What we feel we need and what satisfies our needs are inflated well beyond what is actually required to live a good and satisfying life. We buy much more than enough stuff. Directly or indirectly, the stuff we buy consumes finite natural resources on which our lives ultimately depend.[111]

We now live in an age where we suffer from such an array of ailments not merely restricted to the physical, psychological or the physiological but ways of thinking that seem to impact upon our lives more so than even before, where even the smallest stress has us seeking doctors, counsellors, therapists, coaches, mentors and so on and so on. I've put in 'so on and so on' because I can't think of anything more, but it sounds like I could if push came to shove and 'so on and so on' always sounds better than 'etc., etc.'. In her book *Laugh your way to Happiness*, Lesley Lyle makes a similar point,

It has become a rarity today to see someone smile and laugh with gay abandon. It seems as if people have forgotten how to laugh. In this competitive high-pressure and high-tension world, laughter is fast disappearing and people are succumbing to daily stressors that relentlessly rob them of the ability to laugh.[112]

She also highlights in her book that the majority of adults are 'estimated to laugh an average of 15 times a day, unlike children who laugh and giggle between 300–500 times each day'[113] (no wonder kids never get around to cleaning their room) which is a staggering statistic, but will no doubt resonate with any adult. She goes on to make the point that 'humans learn to laugh long before they walk or talk'. We may not ever laugh 300 times a day ever again but joking aside, the point that we lose something as we move from childhood into adulthood, I don't think any of us could disagree with.

In Maurice Charney's *Comedy: A Geographic and Historical Guide*, Wake Forest philosopher Adrian Bardon, writes

Humor is explained by human beings' special conceptual abilities. The pursuit of humor represents a kind of play that contributes to conceptual flexibility. The feeling associated with this kind of play is amusement... (Humor) actually helps sharpen our ability to respond to cognitively challenging situations. This would also explain why adults tend to demand more clever and subtle humor than children do: One needs humor of increasing subtlety and complexity in order to challenge one's cognitive flexibility, and humor can only be funny when it does this.[114]

Lesley Lyle makes some important points including that no one can laugh without smiling – bet you just smiled, now you're chuckling to yourself. In her book, Lesley opens her chapter on smiling with a quote from Phyllis Diller, 'A smile is a curve that sets everything straight.' What a wonderful quote!

She highlights differences between fake and genuine smiles, talks about the importance and benefits of half-smiles, the effects on your vocal cords and tone when you smile and even refers to research by the British Dental Association whereby one smile can generate the same brain stimulation as '2, 000 bars of chocolate and be equal to receiving up to £16, 000 in cash!' *So* for those of you who have a 'sweet tooth', knock it on the head, just smile instead! Every time you think of Dairy Milk, Mars, Kit Kat, or Twix just smile and say I'm not going there.

Why should we look to humour?

Humour permeates every facet of life, it's free, it surrounds us, it's with us every day, and everyone has it or can access it, even in the darkest moments, in the challenges that life throws at us there are moments of humour. It's on a par with many other art forms (as we see by the many thousands of people who throng to see comedians in 'concert' on a regular basis), it has been immortalised in graffiti throughout the ages, it's a dominant feature in social media; television, radio and film, it has reached cult status and in my own profession (youth work – did I mention that yet?) it is a tool or mechanism used by many to engage a variety of audiences, e.g., comedians, political commentators, teachers, etc.

> Laughter is your birthright, a natural part of life that is innate and inborn. Infants begin smiling during the first weeks of life and laugh out loud within months of being born. Even if you did not grow up in a household where laughter was a common sound, you can learn to laugh at any stage of life.[115]

Training programmes, conferences, seminars (and similar) in comedy, happiness and humour are not uncommon. There are even institutes across the world set up for this very purpose, an example being the Centre for Comedy Studies Research at Brunel University in London; and with the advent of social media, we are bombarded, of course, with humourous images, messages, and videos every day with Facebook and YouTube, just two among the many well-recognised mechanisms at our disposal.

Humour is of course a spontaneous reaction or natural consequence to a given situation, but we also know it's a powerful tool that if used properly and accordingly can achieve major results. Kevin Daum in his article, '8 Ways Using Humor Will Make You a Better Leader' lends weight to this notion when (paraphrased) he states that 'humour energises people, it creates lasting memories, breaks the tension, puts things in perspective, livens things up, disarms an uncomfortable situation, builds a bonded community and makes people feel great'.[116]

And if anyone thought that Humour could not be a force for change, they need not look any further than Iceland where in 2009, comedian Jon Gnarr helped to form the 'Best Party' and won 34.7% of the vote at the 2010 municipal elections. He became Mayor and helped to turn around the fortunes of Iceland from near bankruptcy to a once again thriving economy. Yip, politicians, and bankers screwed up the economy and a comedian fixed it, isn't that ironic? No, you don't have to answer the question... it was more a comment. More recently we have seen Ukrainian President Volodymyr Zelensky, a former comedian, show extraordinary leadership during Russia's invasion of Ukraine. There's a lot to be said for those with a sense of humour being able to exhibit effective leadership.

Health Benefits

I've already touched upon the health benefits of humour earlier and I'm certainly not for one second saying that if you laugh a lot continuously you will always be in good health, I mean you've probably often heard people use the term 'I died laughing', which is of course suggests or certainly implies they laughed so hard that fell into a semi-conscious state, although in Northern Ireland that can take on a different meaning altogether but it's clear, laughing is good for you.

There are of course some health problems that no matter how much you laugh or have laughed in the past you need clear medical intervention, but for the average punter like you and I, laughing has many benefits.

Laughing works out the diaphragm, abdominal, respiratory, facial, leg, and back muscles and is estimated by scientists that laughing 100 times equals the same physical exertion as a 10-minute workout on a rowing machine or 15 minutes on a stationary exercise bike. So only 98 laughs to go...!

How many times have you laughed so much that your side was sore, or sides were 'splitting'? Well, essentially, that means there are muscles you haven't been exercising and if you haven't been exercising them before, you need to start. So, laughing hard, which of course is free and costs nothing can exercise muscles that you might have spent a fortune on when signing up to a gym to exercise.

William Fry, a pioneer on laughter research, in an article for WebMD was said to indicate that it took ten minutes on a rowing machine for his heart rate to reach the level it would after just one minute of hearty laughter.

Without sounding like stating the obvious, but to state the obvious, in order to laugh you, of course, need a sense of humour. Aside from the physical benefits there are psychological, emotional, and social benefits.

Humour can also help you be more spontaneous, be less defensive, release inhibitions and be more honest with your feelings, it also helps you shift perspective, i.e., see things in a different light.

How often have you spoken with someone about a serious issue and ended up making light of it or cracking a few jokes about the situation and came away from it looking at things in a different way? Yes? And your friend comes away thinking, flip, the next time I won't be so quick to answer the phone!

It also combats fear, comforts you, helps you to relax, spreads happiness, cultivates optimism, helps communication.[117] Even those who have experienced adversity can find humour as it can help acknowledge and dispel negative emotions and strengthen social support among people who have come through trauma and challenges. It can also be a way for people who have survived a difficult experience to mentor and encourage those who are still going through it.[118]

According to Craig Zelizer, 'Humour can be used to help groups deal with tensions, release frustrations, and also heal mental and emotional wounds. The use of humour for releasing emotions that have built up as a result of conflicts can be particularly important to help groups cope and maintain their sanity.'[119]

James O'Dea puts it another way,

> The effervescence of laughing and coming together and then surrendering from there to a deeper joy of collaboration gives us the taste of the huge richness of this subject for peace-building. When we are plugged into the primal and unifying field of connection, for which laughter is an obvious but not exclusive door, our body and mind reward us with a cascading flow of inner delight that spreads to others.[120]

Humour is an underlying character trait associated with the positive emotions used in the broaden-and-build theory of cognitive development. Research investigating the psycho-neuroimmunological effects (interaction between the nervous and immune systems) of laughter has found that there is a strong relationship between good health and good humour.

Psychologist Steve Sultanoff, PhD., who is the president of the Association for Applied and Therapeutic Humor, offers this explanation:

> With deep, heartfelt laughter, it appears that serum cortisol, which is a hormone that is secreted when we're under stress, is decreased. So when you're having a stress reaction, if you

laugh, apparently the cortisol that has been released during the stress reaction is reduced.[121]

Studies at the University of Maryland found that when a group of people were shown a comedy, after the screening their blood vessels performed normally, whereas when they watched a drama, after the screening their blood vessels tended to tense up and restricted the blood flow. Studies also show stress decreases the immune system.

Some studies have shown that humor may raise infection-fighting antibodies in the body and boost the levels of immune cells. When we laugh, natural killer cells which destroy tumors and viruses increase, along with Gamma-interferon (a disease-fighting protein), T-cells (important for our immune system) and B-cells (which make disease-fighting antibodies). As well as lowering blood pressure, laughter increases oxygen in the blood, which also encourages healing.[122]

Rob Gee, leads improvisation and sketch workshops with primary school children and tell us that,

Some teachers run scared of allowing comedians to teach their kids, but they shouldn't be so sceptical. Why not? Think of what a huge problem it is getting boys to read and write. When I teach kids about sketch comedy, they love to write down their sketch ideas. It's one of the few times you can see them enjoying writing. So learning how to do sketches helps improves their literacy, their confidence, their self-esteem.... It's the antithesis of the traditionalist view of what should be happening in schools, but given that most of the jobs that our kids will be doing in the next 50 years haven't been invented yet, it seems important to train kids to be flexible, have self-esteem, be literate, rather than follow a traditional curriculum – comedy can help with those things.[123]

So there you are, I rest my case, your honour. Okay, seriously, which given the topic seems a little ironic to say that but it's clear, laughter is good for you, very good for you. The expression 'laughter is the best medicine', is not merely an expression. So next time someone tells you to stop laughing, use the opportunity to have a conversation with him or her about the benefits of laughter and the importance of having a sense of humour... unless of course you've just been arrested, or someone has a gun pointing at you.

Why don't we laugh as much as we did before?

We live in a world now where we seem to be continuously under pressure, where everything seems so much faster, stress is greater, answers are sought quicker and where we seem to have not only less time overall, but even less time to stop and reflect, to take stock, to smile even, or to laugh.

There are many reasons we don't laugh as much as we did before and it's not for the lack of comedians, sitcoms, theatre, social media and so on, but rather I'm talking about our capacity for laughter, our ability to make space for humour and having humour as a state of mind.

In keeping with the theme of this competitive, high-pressure, and high-tension world and perhaps why we laugh much less than we have than in previous generations, I have outlined below what I view as a list of modern-day stresses.

They don't constitute any kind of official paper, nor do they have roots in scientific or medical studies, nor do they represent the views of anyone other than my own musings. They're, of course, designed more to evoke discussion as well as highlight what I believe is the need for more humour in our lives.

- **Time Scarcity**: We never have enough time to do anything – we always have other things to do
- **Information Saturation**: We are saturated everyday with information from every angle – 24-hour Television, Radio, Advertising, Newspapers, social media, etc.
- **Attention Poverty**: We hear constant complaints of not getting enough attention or we are not being heard or no one is listening
- **Instant Gratification**: We are not prepared to wait anymore; we want things, and we want them now
- **Validation Starvation**: Our achievements and accomplishments fail to be recognised – we don't get the validation we feel we are entitled to
- **Resilience Passivism**: We seem to buckle at the latest signs of pressure – our resilience is tested on a seemingly more regular basis than ever before, and many seem unable to fight to remain resilient becoming almost passive to the challenges faced
- **Self-help Explosion**: Bookshops, social media and television seem to be filled with products to help you help yourself as we seem to have lost our ability to deal with challenges and address issues in our lives – we are constantly reminded we need to be fixed
- **Connection Disconnection**: Advances in technology has enabled us to be more connected than ever before yet we spend that much time in front of screens or with our heads facing downwards that we have become disconnected with those around us, next to us, beside us and so on
- **Perspective Paralysis**: We seem to have lost or lose perspective on many issues – we over-estimate or exaggerate, we seem to lose sight of how things are in reality, our ability to maintain perspective seems to have been paralysed by events or other people

- **Values Deconstruction:** Many of the values we hold or have held have been deconstructed as society evolves and we try to make sense of the world as we learn how to deal with change
- **Diversity Sensationalism:** Diversity has been sensationalised in the media creating fear and panic about certain groups
- **Mental Congestion:** We have seemingly much more to think about and many more decisions to make thus blocking or inhibiting our ability to think and rationalise
- **Situational Escapism:** Such is the pressures of life that we seek to find solace away from everyday pressures where we can 'escape' to other situations thus not dealing with realities we actually face
- **Punishment Obsession:** We live in a society that is keen to punish everyone who commits any kind of wrong – legal or otherwise – we don't want to see anyone 'get off' even if it makes the situation worse, we all have a clear sense of justice, and that justice must be exercised to deter others
- **Activism Burnout:** Such are the images and messages that come to us by so many more mediums than before that we have grown 'tired' in many ways of taking a stand against things we might have rallied at in the past
- **Responsibility Negligence:** We have become very good at asserting our rights but eerily woeful at acknowledging and assuming our responsibilities – it's much easier to profess our rights than to take stock and reflect on what our responsibilities are as this might require some level of thinking and of course this takes time and energy, and we might just end up losing face in the process if we have to reconsider and acknowledge what we know to be true
- **Righteousness Affirmation:** Being wrong or having to say sorry is something that we find more and more difficult

and thus we always aim to be right or look to others to affirm how right we are rather than entertain the idea of others critiquing our sense of being right in order to help us be more thoughtful

- **Humility Depreciation**: We seem to have forgotten about the importance of humility, about treating people with a little more respect, treating people as we would have ourselves treated
- **Fixation Intervention**: Rather than working on transforming systems and processes we have become fixated with fixing things – we never seem to take the long-term view but rather always looking for short-term fixes
- **Happiness Mythology**: We're always being encouraged to look for a state of happiness and thus creating an impression that it is always something that must be sought, got and found whereby merely aiming for contentment will enable us reach greater levels of happiness
- **Complexity Overload**: We seem to have developed the knack for complicating matters rather than adopting simple approaches, we always seem to want to come up with new ways of re-inventing, redrawing, or adding to the wheel rather than just keeping it simple
- **Spotlight Magnification**: When we put the spotlight on a range of issues, concerns and fears we seem to magnify them beyond that what we need to thus we create even more stress and worry.

So, after all that, what's our key message, you ask?

Well, it's quite simple, Health is a major contribution to Well Being and Humour is a major contribution to health so please 'buy' into this and share the humour message! Come join us on our journey to spread laughter and joy. Know and understand the power of humour!

37. The problem with absolutes is exactly that – they are absolute

There's a story about people on a boat. A guy decides to dig through the floor of his cabin. Water flows in. Other passengers are pissed. But it's his own cabin, the guy argues, so why should it matter? Personal choice only goes so far when we're all on the same boat.
Unknown

In one of the Star Wars films, I think it's *Revenge of the Sith*, Mace Windu in his battle with the Sith Lord, Darth Sidious, aka Governor Palpatine, utters the words, 'only a Sith deals in absolutes'; clearly the message to take from this is that being absolute means something bad, or evil, or certainly not behaving like a Jedi, who traditionally stands for good.

It is of course a film, and only one line but the line has always stuck with me – the behaviour of Darth Sidious, and his apprentice, Anakin Skywalker aka Darth Vader, would suggest, that there was no in-between, that things are very much black and white, and compromise, accommodation or middle ground wasn't on any page in the Dark Side play book.

Absolutes are often associated with people as a negative trait. In some ways it's neither negative nor positive, it's just a trait, and its consequence depends on the situation, and the person receiving or delivering the message. If someone is trying to beat you up, you can be absolute that you're not going to accept that scenario, unless of course you feel that you cannot do anything about it or that you are deserving of it, but by and large, even if you are unable to defend yourself, for whatever reason, it is highly unlikely you accept it.

Absolutes, of course, tend to refer more to ideas, concepts, opinion, thoughts, views, values, and beliefs, and even the most caring, open, warm, and welcoming people can be absolute about anything. I have met people who would take the coat of their back for you but might have absolute views on things like marriage is something that is between a man and woman only, or that there should be stricter border controls, or most recently, that Covid isn't real, or when you support BLM (Black Lives Matter) they respond with All Lives Matter and no matter how much you try to explain the rationale behind BLM, they are still steadfast in their beliefs that 'All Lives Matter'.

One of the problems with growing up in Ireland, and in particular Northern Ireland, is that most of us were brought up to believe in absolutes – absolutes connected with religion, identity, nationality, and culture among other things. And even though Northern Ireland tends to be a relatively peaceful place now, or as I tend to say, we've stopped killing each other, many of the absolutes still exist, not least of all because over 90% of our population live apart from one another, i.e., in segregated areas, and the same applies to our schooling, where approximately only 7% of our school-going population attends integrated schools, across both primary and secondary education.

Personally, I find absolutes so restrictive, for example, if you sign up to a particular set of beliefs, there is a danger you become lumbered with them. And because you have taken them on as part of your identity, it's exceedingly hard to get shot of them, and any reflection on them means accepting painful or uncomfortable truths, and therefore, the easiest thing is not to confront this, but continue to defend your beliefs.

We've seen this with various politicians such as Trump, Putin, Bolsonaro, and Erdogan among others. They stick to certain beliefs and opinions, even when evidence counters this, and refuse to contemplate any other reality. And in doing so, they become absolute. And this of course is the problem – the inability to change or rather the unwillingness to do so.

Over the last number of years, I have discovered from quite a few people I know, very absolute views about a range of issues – Covid and BLM most notably. This has surprised me – my expectations of them were different, but of course it's in these moments we learn about the values that people hold and whether we wish to maintain that friendship.

As someone who was once a right-wing conservative Catholic, I was quite absolute about many things. As someone that is now a secular humanist, I realise how restrictive absolutes become. There's not much I'm absolutist about these days – I tend to have a scientific mindset, where if new information becomes available then it's time to review the old beliefs. I'm what Steven D'Souza, Dianna Renner might describe as an 'uncertaintist', where their motto is 'never be absolute'.

There is a danger in being absolute, not necessarily that from your neighbour who sticks firmly to certain beliefs, but those that are already in power. It doesn't even have to be those in charge of powerful nations such as those individuals already mentioned but in countries where infrastructure or governance is limited, e.g., Afghanistan. As Timothy Taylor warns,

> science directly challenges ideologs who need their followers to believe them infallible. We should not underestimate the glamour and influence of anti-science ideologies. Left unchecked, they could usher in a new intellectual Dark Age. That is what happened in Nigeria.... Boko Haram maintains we inhabit a flat, 6, 000-year-old Earth and that the disk-shaped sun, which is smaller, passes over it daily. Heresy (such as belief in evolution, or that rain is predicated on evaporation) can lead to a judgement of apostasy, which is punished by death. Reason having fled, the people are increasingly struggling with malnutrition, drought, and disease.'[124]

Being absolute, in my opinion, is to deny yourself of many things. It removes so many opportunities and possibilities because your actions are informed by your set of beliefs and therefore, things you might contemplate doing but feel you can't or at least can't be seen to be doing, or expressing even, means you cannot experience whatever it might be, and therefore, absolutes are not such a good thing.

. By being absolute you learn only to defend and to support, and you tend not to question or reflect, and for me this is a shame. I want to know, I want to learn, I want to evolve, I want to grow and if we are absolute, we are denied opportunities to do this. I believe that my journey in life, or rather my obligation and responsibility whilst I remain on Earth, is to keep learning.

I want to know why things are the way they are; I want to know why things work the way they do, why people behave in the manner they do, why random situations and events happen and so on. And the only way for me to do this is to be everything but absolute – yes, I might debate and discuss, and I do, but not from the perspective of drawing my own conclusions but because of all the work that others have done to uncover answers to questions that have challenged humanity over millennia.

Being absolute is debilitating.

38. Don't aim for happiness, aim for contentment

Happiness is where you are now, or nowhere at all. It's not a new relationship, it's not a new job, it's not a completed goal, and it's not a new car. Until you give up on the idea that happiness is somewhere else, it will never be where you are.
Unknown

Happiness is an illusion! Okay, it's a bit of a dramatic statement but there is an element of truth, let me explain why. People often talk about wanting to be happy, or at least happier, as if happiness were something to achieve, or a state of mind to work towards or a place that you need to get to.

That for me is why it is somewhat of an illusion. This is not to suggest you can't be happy, or even happy continuously (who hasn't met someone that doesn't seem to be in a continuous state of happiness or positivity) but it is just not possible to be happy all the time. It takes time, energy, and a certain degree of conviction.

Being happy is of course relative – you can have 'everything' yet still be unhappy. In fact, research has shown, that when you reach a certain level of wealth, for example, the difference that having a little extra (when you already have a lot) makes is less than having a whole lot when you have nothing. If a millionaire earns £10, 000 in interest over a month, it won't make any difference to him, but give £10, 000 to someone who has a balance of £100 in their account, and you can be sure he or she will be much happier.

But this idea, that permeates in the West in particular, i.e., you'll be happier if you have the beautiful partner, the big house, the new car, the annual holidays, the weekends away and more, creates the impression, that happiness is something to be achieved, and therefore if you don't achieve it, you invariably become less happy, even unhappy, or even depressed.

'Happiness is such an illusory thing that spending too much time chasing it is not very worthwhile'[125] Richard Templar tells us. Matt Avery makes the point that, 'It is easy, and commonplace, to work hard in the pursuit of something that you hope will bring you happiness, without ever stopping to take stock of whether what you are doing is likely to result in what you are trying to achieve, and if so, whether it is a prudent and efficient means of doing so.'[126]

Research has demonstrated that our traditional notions of happiness are often misplaced – 'in 2003, two psychologists, Tom Gilarich & Leaf Van Boven collaborated on a landmark study.... The results were clear, the conclusion simple: experiences do make people happier than material possessions'[127] whilst 'one of the happiest countries in the world (coming in at number 14) is Costa Rica. That's despite the fact that it is only the 77th wealthiest, with a per-capita income of $15, 000.'[128]

I was never materialistic – having somewhere to live that is warm, and where the fundamentals required to get by are in place, or, for example, having a car that essentially gets me from A to B is what is most important in my opinion – as long as under the bonnet doesn't let me down, it doesn't have to shine on the outside.

I of course still wanted to achieve, especially in my career. I wanted to secure certain positions in certain fields, I wanted to be recognised for what I had done or what I might do, and there were moments when that didn't happen. I often felt that I had fallen short at the wrong moment, or there are times I'd see other people in certain positions of authority or they'd have achieved something, and I might wonder how they got there, or how they managed that and similar.

I wasn't jealous of them, it was more about myself, how I had 'failed', rather than resent people getting where they got to, but over the last number of years, I have learned to stop thinking this way, often spending little or no time wondering about these things.

I have in many ways become content with my lot – that doesn't mean lacking ambition, or putting goals aside, or not wanting to still achieve, but these days I am for contentment, as opposed to trying to be happy or achieve a state of happiness that exists somewhere in my mind.

A number of years back I secured the 'ideal job' but it didn't turn out the way I had imagined so much so that I walked away from it – the degree of responsibility and authority I had was immense and a beautiful pay grade – I thought I had finally 'arrived' after some years of bouncing between jobs, freelancing and bidding for work, and here I was, finally in the moment I wanted to be, and I loved being there, not in an arrogant way, just in a very happy place, content with what I had achieved.

After a short period, things begun to happen – 'forces' were at work behind the scenes, and before long I said to myself, nope, I don't need this, it's not what I came here for, this is not a 'battle' I'm going to win, and I became very content about it, and handed in my notice, and left.

Walking away from it was liberating – in fact, I had no other job to go to, but I was okay with it. I believed in myself enough to make it work, even though everything was uncertain, and I hadn't exactly the most buoyant of bank balances you could ever find.

The happiness I was looking for in that job never materialised, and so contentment in recent times has become my goal. This event was just one of many in the last decade where I made decisions about just being content. For about 10 years or more, I was heavily involved in international youth work and really enjoyed this, and at one point I was part of UK National Agency's Erasmus+ Pool of Trainers and Assessors – and I enjoyed this – there were nice 'gigs' (work) when you could get them.

After a while, though, I realised it was time to end that relationship and I did – this was during a period when I was freelancing, and much uncertainty followed. Again, I thought I will find a way to survive and did.

During these few years, I had decided to stop putting myself through the chore of applying for jobs and bidding or tendering for work endlessly and concentrate on the things I liked doing and the things I wanted to do, but of course also finding a way to generate income that keeps things ticking over but which creates space for me to focus on what it is I wanted to do.

And since then, that's what I have concentrated on – even finding time to write this book. Now I appreciate that not everyone is in a position to do so, and, of course, my kids are now fully-grown adults, and at the time of writing, two of them are already parents themselves, and so the day-to-day pressures of meeting the needs of family have passed, at least financially speaking.

Rolf Dobelli offers a useful piece of advice – 'it's important to give a wide berth to tips and advice from self-help authors. For billions of people, these pieces of advice are unlikely to help. But because the unhappy don't write self-help books about failures, the fact remains hidden.'[129]

My key message in this is about altering your thinking from one of perpetually chasing happiness, to one of focusing on the things, situations, events, and people that make you content. Ironically, contentment creates the happiness that people often look for and so if there is one key defining message and most importantly, one lesson I would share with you, it is to aim for contentment and happiness will come!

39. Learn to tell people what you need, what you need to happen or need not to happen, rather than what you want

Your worst enemy cannot harm you as much as your own thoughts, unguarded. But, once mastered, no one can help you as much, not even your father or your mother.
From the book *The Coddling of the American Mind*

It is very easy to end up in an argument, even without trying. I have often ended up in one before I even realised I was in it. And it's just not about disagreeing or trying to prove something. Someone can say something, and you become offended and rather than checking, you immediately assume they are having a go at you.

As someone once said, we listen to reply rather than listen to hear, or something akin to this. When I first heard this expression, I was honest enough with myself to accept that I had often done this, and since hearing or reading this expression, I have genuinely endeavoured to listen to hear as opposed to listening to reply. Not always easy I'll be the first to admit, in fact, very frustrating at times, but most certainly worth practising.

To do so is not just about trying to relieve yourself of your ego, but to really try and get what the other person is saying or the place they are coming from – you might still conclude that they are talking bullshit but at least you can content yourself that you know they're taking bullshit!

That, of course, is not my point – in arguments, discussions, debates, or even polite conversations we often put ourselves first, not always, and not everyone, but we are much more prone to it than we think. There are those that are capable of such immense empathy, that they can run the risk of being completely taken advantage of. But for most of us, we tend to start from a position of ego and I'm not talking about being rude, ignorant, or selfish, but we tend to think about our needs first and foremost.

Let me offer an example, if you get on a bus would you prefer to sit or remain standing to keep a seat free for someone else who might need it more than you? Or if you drive into a car park, do you aim to park closer to the shop door or go to the end of the car park to allow others to have access to one of the spaces near the shop? Of if you join a queue do you suddenly let the next six people behind you get served first as a kind gesture?

Yes, I know these examples might seem simplistic in their thinking but they do demonstrate that we will endeavour to do what's best for us ahead of others, unless of course there is good reason to put others first – your children or your elderly parents, for example, or a friend in need, or making time for a new work colleague because you remembered how nervous you were on your first day.

Or you know of someone short of cash, but you need that money to get by to the end of the month and so you could help them on the promise of getting it back, but it is a risk, and so if you decide not to help him or her, it's perfectly understandable, even if you feel guilty about it.

My point is that our starting point is often misplaced, or we approach it from the wrong place. We react to someone, or we tell people what we want or would like, as opposed to telling people what we need. How often do you calmly but assertively tell people, this is what I need, as opposed to simply asserting what you want?

You might not literally say 'this is what I want', but if your response communicates to someone what you expect is such and such, then they respond in a similar fashion, and before you know it, you're at loggerheads, or have got yourself into a position, that is hard to get out of without losing face.

For the last number of years, I have been doing some freelance work as an External Supervisor with staff from Youth Work

Ireland. It's very enjoyable work and I really have appreciated the opportunity to work with some wonderful human beings as well as Youth Work Ireland Tipperary.

One common theme is that all staff have encountered challenges when working with other staff or volunteers on a variety of issues – this is perfectly normal – humans of course can be hard work, they are the sum of their experiences and present themselves in all sorts of ways.

It's always interesting to hear from individuals their accounts of the situations they are facing and how they have dealt with them thus far. They require certain things, and often have tried different ways of communicating to 'the others' what they are looking for. Each time I have posed the question, 'have you told them what you need?' It's always an interesting question because the response tends to be the same – no!

In some ways it's surprising that people don't try this but, in many ways, it isn't that surprising – we're not so used to telling people what we need – it's almost as if it is a sign of weakness but it's almost revolutionary.

If you begin with the word need it changes the focus and shapes the conversation in terms of how that person can help you as opposed to what you want. And who doesn't want to help someone in need, even if it's only not to react to them, or if only just to listen to what they have to say.

I can't recall when, but some years ago, when I first realised this, it was a bit of a revelation – quite simply, tell people what you need, and everything is framed differently. It's almost viewed as a request, it shows that you value and respect the person enough to consult or ask or seek permission from them without having to phrase it that way, which I accept can of course sound a little like you're pleading with them, or even begging them.

Understandably, no one wants to appear like that, but if you get the result you want, and you appear to be humbler to the other person, and that person views you in a more positive light, then why not. People like to help, and they want to be known for helping – at least in my experience anyways.

The word 'need' is completely undervalued – when we talk about need, we almost always see it through the prism of others, i.e., their needs, rather than simply saying to others, here are my needs, and here is what I need from you. Can you help or support me? It changes the conversation entirely, like who wants to refuse someone who is in need. It's not a sign of weakness, it's a powerful strategy.

Begin with what you need – a pre-emptive strike as it were and being assertive becomes a whole lot easier.

40. Your expectations of people will determine whether you are going to like them, so revise your expectation — it will save you a shit-load of grief

When you love someone, you love the person as they are, and not as you'd like them to be.
Leo Tolstoy

It's very hard to find anyone on the planet that has no expectation of anything – that is an expectation in itself. It might be stating the obvious, but everyone has differing expectations of people, things, situations, all of which are influenced by the environment we grow up in, our upbringing, the culture we form part of, the country we live in, the people we socialise with, the work we do or the schools we attend, as well as the things we hear on TV and Radio, stories we read in newspapers, the internet and on social media, among many other things.

Our expectations are built around the values and beliefs we possess, the principles we adhere too, the experiences we have had, and sometimes the mood we are in, in each moment. They are not limited to this or what I describe above, but a factor common among all of this, is that we tend to think our expectations are normal, are correct, are in line with most other people, and on discovering this not to be the case, we don't tend to look at this being a problem with us, but rather others.

When the expectations of others contrast with our own or crash right up against them, our natural reaction is to assume that the other person has got it wrong, that they must be thinking differently, or that they are ill-informed, or at least misinformed. Rarely, do we consider our expectations as the problem. This is particularly prevalent if we are surrounded by people who tend to look like us, think like us, speak like us, share the same opinion, values, and beliefs, and have similar if not mirror-like experiences.

They say travel broadens the mind and it most certainly does because inevitably you meet people different to yourself and therefore you are challenged, critiqued, tested, and questioned about the expectations you have, and you must learn how to respond accordingly. That kind of experience brings you to the point of reflecting upon your own expectations, and you begin to realise it's your expectations that come into focus.

Over the years, and particularly when I was younger, in part because of my own upbringing and what I would describe as indoctrination into Catholicism, I had expectations of others, which were essentially that you need to think like me and share my beliefs otherwise I looked upon you differently.

It was quite a self-righteous way to be and to be honest, not very nice, but at the time, I didn't really know any better, and wanted to become the person I thought I should be, partly to honour my parents. Thankfully, much of that has changed over the years, and I swung 180 degrees in the other direction. What has changed even more so in my adult life is my expectations of others, and ultimately, I now have put the focus on my expectations and have consciously endeavoured to change them, not to something else, but rather, alter my thinking towards other people.

I no longer have great expectations of people if truth be told, not in a can't trust them or they disappoint me kind of way, but rather in a *I'm no longer going to build up expectations so that I won't be disappointed kind of way*. People are people, they can behave in all sorts of ways, some that seem quite common, but also, others that seem out of the ordinary, those that are not so common. I have also changed my expectations of others because I appreciate much more that I need to be realistic about what to expect. We live in an era where people are much more inclined not to review their ideas, or reflect upon their actions or behaviours, and much less likely to accept alternative viewpoints. And therefore, unless you have a positive relationship with someone where the potential for meaningful conversation and discussion is possible, there's a distinct lack of opportunity in this era to engage people without it escalating into an argument.

David Mc Rainey offers some useful insight as to why it is more pervasive now than ever before – he talks about the *Just-World fallacy* and the *Forer effect*. The Forer Effect is 'the tendency to believe vague statements.... When you need something to be true, you will look for patterns, you connect the dots like the stars of a constellation. Your brain abhors disorder... your capacity to fool yourself is greater than the abilities of any conjurer, and conjurers come in many guises. You are a creature compelled to hope'.[130]

The Just-World fallacy 'helps you to build a false sense of security. You want to feel in control, so you assume as long as you avoid bad behaviour, you won't be harmed.... Deep down, you want to believe hard work and virtue will lead to success, and evil and manipulation will lead to ruin, so you go ahead and edit the world to match those expectations. Yet, in reality, evil often prospers and never pays the price.... The just-world fallacy tells them fairness is built into the system, and so they rage when the system unbalances karmic justice'.[131]

When individuals have fixed beliefs like this it makes it difficult to convince or persuade them of anything else and therefore having expectations of bringing people to a different place as it were, is to expend energy and time in the false hope they can change. In this situation, it is not they that have to change, it is you, you must review your expectations.

How might you do this? Well, if you have made it to this point in the book, you will already know that one of my mottos/ mantras is, 'it is what it is' which is for me, the ultimate escape clause and prevents me from getting worked up too much about anything, it allows me to be okay with 'stuff' and helps me manage my expectations.

The ultimate secret in all of this is not so much your expectations of others but knowing your own expectations and how you can manage them. If you can begin to manage your own expectations, particularly regarding others, you win! You will be able to tailor your behaviour and temper your reactions, with a more relaxed, easy-going, and calm approach.

It really is a good way to be – these days I tend to only get 'worked up' about minimal things, such as my laptop not performing, or if I don't manage my time carefully and I'm running late and stress a little about disappointing people with my timekeeping, but I find a way to control or reconcile this with my own inner voices.

Aside from this, being able to transform a mindset from one that projects expectation onto others to one that is about managing my own expectation of myself, is transformational. You become more relaxed, more chilled, happier, more patient, more amenable to others, less stressed, angry, or anxious, and arguably healthier, as the expectations you hold of others dissipates and are re-routed into your own mindset.

As a result, you only need to think about yourself most of the time and therefore move away from concerning yourself with the words, deeds, and actions of others. Try it, liberate your mind by removing your expectations of others, you don't need it in your life. Let go, let it go, grab some freedom. Tailor your expectations to ground zero level and watch the stress dissipate.

41. We are driven by a need to have purpose and it's damaging

If outside validation is your only sources of nourishment, you will be hungry for the rest of your life.
Unknown

It might be stating the obvious, (I might have said that already in this book – apologies!) but we are driven by the need to have purpose, including the feeling (even if it goes against our own instinct) that we must compete with our peers, friends, family, and colleagues to achieve.

My belief is that we have become stuck on a constant journey of exploring, designing, and producing endless shiny, sophisticated new tools, not only those of a physical kind, but tools of all varieties, e.g., methodologies, approaches, concepts, models of practice, and so on, so much so that we overlook the more important things in life, i.e., conversing, being present, listening, supporting, reaching out. We are so busy doing that we often simply forget about 'being', e.g., we don't create enough spaces for things like conversations and just being present with others.

A reminder from Lesson 31 – many of the reasons why we are here is down to a seemingly embedded ethos of individualism, endless competition, a lack of solidarity, a growing distrust of current and historical systems of governance and mainstream institutions, managed exploitation of individuals, imbalanced lifestyles, pointless priorities, constant measurements, 'the binary' mindset and the growth of the 'Fix You' Mentality.

William Davies gives us a hint of the times we live in:

Twenty-four-hour news channels display real-time financial market reports. Companies employ futurists, trend-spotters and horizon-scanners to imagine what might bubble up next. A surging management consultancy industry and outsourcing of research reduce the need for companies to maintain expertise internally.... In these conditions, individuals must focus less on seeking truth or objectivity, and more on being adaptable.... Education becomes less significant for the knowledge that it provides than for how it contributes to the employability of the recipient, which is as much about attitude, flexibility and technical skills as it is about traditional intellectual or professional vocations.... Rumour offers far more potential for profit than published fact. The context for every life choice is that of competition, how to distinguish oneself from rivals, by qualifications, image-making and management of oneself.... Academic life is accelerated, with new pressures to publish and/or patent research findings more quickly, so as to claim ownership over a subject area before anyone else.[132]

There is plenty of evidence to support his assertions:

- 'we have been induced [or is it seduced]... to accept a vicious ideology of extreme competition, a case of winner takes all'[133]
- 'most of us are wired to want continually to level up, to score higher than others'[134]
- 'we've been conditioned to believe in the myth that evolution is about competition'[135]
- 'a moral and spiritual vacuum is yet again filled with anarchic expressions of individuality, and mad quests for substituted religions and modes of transcendence'[135]
- 'we communicate through our purchases, the facades on our homes, or the numbers in our bank accounts'[137]
- 'our whole society is set on "transmit" and "compete" all the time, seldom on "receive" or "cooperate"'

- 'there is a reason that feedback and recognition are so highly prized by the new power set... their lives are punctuated (perhaps even defined) by the validation and engagement of others. Every text, every image, every post is a call designed for a response: the drip-drip-drip of dopamine-reward they receive from every heart-shaped like'[138]

- 'it seems that despite all the inclinations towards being sociable and friendly our brain is so concerned with preserving a sense of identity and peace of mind that it makes us willing to screen anyone and anything that could endanger this'[139]

- 'the belief that competition and individualism are humanity's defining features did not arise spontaneously... it was refined in the 20th century by neoliberalism.... It defines us as competitors guided above all other impulses by the urge to get ahead of our fellows'[140]

- 'the just-world fallacy helps you to build a false sense of security. You want to feel in control, so you assume as long as you avoid bad behaviour, you won't be harmed.... Deep down, you want to believe hard work and virtue will lead to success, and evil and manipulation will lead to ruin, so you go ahead and edit the world to match those expectations.'[141]

Yet contrary to this 'all the progress that the human race has achieved in the last few hundred years has been due to people trading and cooperating with one another'.[142]

As a society we are very focused on creating, developing, innovating, changing, amending, re-creating, and re-imagining ourselves to have purpose and to be looked upon as having purpose, or to put it another way, to appear confident, focused and as if you know exactly what you are doing. Paul Gilbert attributes this to 'the Western Capitalist model [which has] very little interest in whether you understand your mind. It will train you in the skills necessary to make you into a contributor towards profit-seeking goals'.[143]

D'Souza and Renner tell us 'an increasing number of us are now in professions where we think for a living… the rank and, power that we can draw from our knowledge and expertise can make us feel important and more worthy. In turn this gives us more confidence'.[144]

We live an era when the pressure to do rather than just be is immense. We're all expected to be creators, developers, initiators, innovators, entrepreneurs – we are driven by a need to have purpose and it forces us to compete, and that's damaging!

42. Context is everything

How long a minute is, depends on what side of the bathroom you're on.
Zall's 2nd Law

Our evolution has been quite distinctive and of course the events that have influenced it, but we now live in a world where our failure to fully appreciate who we are and the journey we have travelled, or to take the opportunity to reflect on where we are at in this moment is costing us. Context is everything and understanding this is vital as we try to get clarity on many of the questions of the modern age.

Let's consider some key moments from the last 70 years. Some of these I have already touched upon but I reference them again to help contextualise developments that help give us some indication of where we have gone wrong and some idea of the challenges we face and how we need to re-think our priorities. Contextualising these events, I believe gives us much greater meaning and I would argue far better perspective which in turn enables us to know the steps we have to take. In this regard I would argue that context is everything:

So, just to recap:

i)   between 1950 and 2000, the global population increased 2.5 times, but food production has more than tripled[145]

ii)   the rise in obesity in recent decades also mirrors the fall in sleep duration and quality[146]

iii) the share of wealth controlled by the top 0.1% grew from 7% in the 1970s to 22% in 2012[147]

iv)   three-quarters of all border walls and fences that currently exist were erected after the year 2000[148]

v) as of 2008, humanity was consuming 30% more per year than the planet sustainably produces[149]

    i) globally, obesity has almost doubled between 1980 and 2014[150]

    ii) today there are 28 cities with a population of more than 10 million people – by 2030, the UN predicts that there will be 41 – and more than half will be in Asia[154]

In addition:

- since 1990, the gap between rich and poor has increased exponentially
- the top one-tenth of the richest 1% own almost as much wealth as the bottom 90%[151]
- by 2008, $4 to $5 of debt was required to create $1 of growth[152]
- 70% of the developed world have experienced stagnation between 2005 and 2014[153]
- incredible developments in IT and social media – launch of eBay (1997), the first Wi-Fi-enabled laptop (a Mac, 1999), broadband (2000), expansion of 3G (2001), MySpace (2003), Facebook (2004) Twitter (2006); iPhone & Kindle (2007), notebook sales overtook Desktop sales (2008), Samsung's first Android phone (2009) iPad (2010), Tumblr, Instagram (2010) and Snapchat (2011) – has seen an vast increase of the speed of life and with it our inability to keep pace with it

We are now in an era, often referred to as the Anthropocene, where we are no longer shaped by our planet, but rather we are shaping the planet. And this brings me to one of the key arguments – Creativity, Imagination, Innovation, and the Entrepreneurial Spirit has brought us to this point – it's a double-edged sword. And there is no sign of us stopping/ slowing down.

And with the likes of India, Brazil, and China endeavouring to catch up with (and in some respects overtake) the West, it's not going to stop anytime soon. The GFN (Global Footprint Network), for example, has calculated that the total amount of productive land and water on Earth amounts to 12 billion global hectares. With roughly 7 billion people on earth, this equates to 1.72 global hectares per person. In 1961 human demand accounted for 0.7 planet's worth of biocapacity.[155]

I alluded to it earlier but, GFN said in 2008, that we needed 1.5 planets to sustain us, something that is clearly unsustainable but worryingly, it is estimated that there are less than 60 harvests left as the Earth's topsoil has been slowly eroded over time due to industrial-scale farming. If we wanted to get an idea of what some of our priorities might be then these offer some indication. But it goes deeper than that.

One factor that can be easily connected to many of the issues in the modern era is a breakdown in or more accurately, the loss of trust. This heavily influences the context we are operating in and in turn impacts future decisions. The more there is a lack of trust in political institutions, the less likely we will be able to get people to work collectively towards any kind of change, never mind positive change.

Rachel Botsman, explores the resulting loss of trust in traditional institutions – 'there are three key, somewhat overlapping, reasons: inequality of accountability (certain people are being punished for wrongdoing while others get a leave pass); twilight of elites and authority (the digital age is flattening hierarchies and eroding faith in experts and the rich and powerful); and segregated echoes chambers (living in our own cultural ghettos and being deaf to other voices).'[156]

William Davies offers some indication as to why this might be: 'As we become more attuned to "real time" events and media, we inevitably end up placing more trust in sensation and emotion than in evidence. Knowledge becomes more valued for its speed and impact than for its cold objectivity, and emotive falsehood often travels faster than fact.... With confidence in the mainstream media also in decline, the power of numbers to facilitate wide-spread agreement and trust is in peril, as very few people have the skills or time to rely on original data sources and expert analysis.'[157]

Douglas Rushkoff offers some thoughts on what is further contributing to this. 'The primary purpose of the internet had changed from supporting a knowledge economy to growing an attention economy. Instead of helping us leverage time to our intellectual advantage, the internet was converted to an "always on" medium, configured to the advantage of those who wanted to market to us or track activities. Going online went from an active choice to a constant state of being.'[158]

Exploring context allows us to become better equipped so as not to jump to conclusions unnecessarily, or that we don't make judgements without due consideration of relevant information. Making time to understand context reveals so much – what was happening at the time, who said what, why, and so on. Without context we don't get the answers we need. Context is EVERYTHING!

43. Giving advice might be more readily accepted if it starts with the words, *What might be helpful is...*

Most people don't listen with intent to understand, they listen with intent to reply.
Stephen R. Covey

In a bid to reassert our place in the world, or to give ourselves a sense of importance, or just to feel that we have value, one thing we often do but not very well is give advice or offer our opinion.

In many ways, this is dangerous, not because what we offer is dangerous but because it can have consequences beyond what we really anticipated. For example, someone recites a story which makes us feel angry and we make some claim about what we would do in the same situation, which does not actually mean we would do it but then we find out said person has just gone and done it and when he or she explains their action it is to your 'advice' they refer to, only to leave you to respond with the words, 'well I didn't actually mean for you to go and do it.' You can probably recall a moment like this from some time in the past.

I grew up in a time with the expression *sticks and stones may break my bones, but words will never hurt me*. This was at a time when we didn't have rolling news, we were limited to a small number of television channels and radio stations, there was no internet and most certainly no social media, and communities were much more cohesive, and there was a greater sense of connection.

I don't want to give the impression that it was all rosy in the garden, or so much easier or very simplistic back then but to a large degree it was – growing up involved going to school (most probably on foot), you came home (which was most likely reasonably close to your school), and you went out and played with your friends – there was no play dates, sleep overs, or being couped up in your room, and when you did go out, you were free to go and explore, and your creative and imaginative senses were tingled, so to speak.

What was very clear is that you spent much less time alone with your thoughts, you were less caring of what people said, you didn't have to check about comments, likes or shares and your fingers were occupied by making and creating things, as opposed to scrolling. When you were bored, you got over it and found a way to occupy yourself, and even if you were on your own part of the time, you imagined and re-imagined.

You also felt part of the community even if you felt a little alone at times, you knew your neighbours, and they knew you, in fact, you knew those that lived in other streets, or down the road. And thus, you had a place, a stake in your community, and you tended to live in the same place for a long time, and thus become almost embedded in your own community. Of course, this is not everyone's experience, and not everyone had such a pleasant upbringing, so I don't look at it through rose-tinted glasses either.

In the modern age now where we are seemingly much less connected for lots of reasons, we are very much in need of feeling part of something, or loved, or cared for, or desired, or at the very least in people's thoughts.

We need to know we mean something to someone(s), that we have value, and when we speak, that it (also) means something, and it can have influence on others. This in turn gives us a sense of self-worth, and with that our self-esteem increases, and the more it increases, the more confident we feel, and in turn we feel more part of society, and so the cycle continues. Of course, it doesn't pan out like this in every case, but it's not far off either. We need to know our words not only have value, but that we are being listened too. This is often a complaint (or an assertion) we hear that people feel they have no voice in this world of noise. Everyone is making noise though, and all too often no one is being heard, or people are trying to be heard over the heads of everyone else. Then there are those that scream silently but that's another issue entirely but is a result of all the noise that goes on around us.

To feel that we have belonging in this world, or be heard, we often are invited, or invite ourselves, sometimes inadvertently, to offer advice, or opinion. Our carefully constructed thoughts or as is often the case, *our unfolding on-the-spot haven't really thought about this, but I don't want to appear not to have an opinion kind of thoughts* are misjudged.

We offer our 'tuppence-worth' based on how we think we might respond, or how we perceive ourselves as responding, even if we have never been in that situation, and as we all too often know, it's not until you are in that situation that you really discover how you would react.

All too often we tend to respond with an assertion – this is what I would do, or this is what I would say – it might be true actually, but that might then only escalate or exacerbate a situation, and then we are 'in it' before we even realise and then not sure how to get out of it, so our challenge is to minimise this kind of scenario arising and get our starting point right.

Easier said than done, of course, but I find simple expressions to use or to keep in mind before responding to any scenario helps navigate moments that can be quite tricky. Often when we offer an opinion, or give advice, we do so from the perspective of how we would imagine ourselves respond which of course is laced with preserving our sense of identity and encased in pride, and this adds an emotional layer (that might not have been present), especially if it's a family member, a friend, or a close colleague from work. We want to show that we care or that we support them and 'have their back'.

But if we are emotionally involved or have a vested interest, we can't be impartial so the best thing we can try and do is talk as if we were in the third person, and rather than responding with the archetypal *well if it were me,* much better to go with *what might be helpful is...* or something along those lines.

In these kinds of situations, it's best to try and detach yourself from your instinct and assume the role of a third party, or someone that has no connection with the person you are supporting. Of course, it is very hard to do, but your choice of words in this moment can have such a bearing on the outcome. It really is important to think carefully about what it is you want to say, and in the end up, what you do say.

Don't offer opinions, offer options, and build those options around what garners the best outcome. You want the person you are supporting to believe they have options, and that they can approach things from the perspective of making better things happen, not choices informed by emotions or a *this is what I would or wouldn't do* approach. Every scenario that someone faces, where they are faced with risks that affect them more than you, is a situation to be treated with the utmost care. What might be helpful in that regard is that when you offer your thoughts you begin with, *what might be helpful is...*

44. When responding to a claim/accusation/insinuation/allegation against you always begin your response with, *Now let me see if I got this straight...*

Clarity is momentum that has no resistance to it.
Abraham Hicks

When responding to a claim/accusation/insinuation/allegation against you always begin your response with, *now let me see if I got this straight* – it buys you thinking time, stops you reacting, clarifies what the other person is saying and 'forces' them to 'put up or shut up'.

If it's a case of 'shut up' then your next response might be to use a bit of humour in response to what they say, e.g., with *just checking* which, of course, can help to de-escalate a potential conflict, and if it's 'put up' then they will either have to back up what they say and then you'll have an idea of what you're dealing with.

Conflict tends to follow a pattern – someone says something, the other person reacts, then an equally terse response follows and so on and before you know, people are knocking lumps out of each other, if not physically, at least verbally, and we know the damage this can do; if only one of them, or at least the person who is initially on the 'receiving end' just asks for clarification it might be so much different.

Those pointing the finger or going on the attack tend to expect a reaction and thus, when a person doesn't react, but seeks clarification, this tends to confuse things, and normally takes the wind out of the sails of those doing the attacking.

In the case where someone needs to back things up, they will have thought about it and explain or justify his or herself, or at the other end of the spectrum he or she go off into a bit of a 'rant' and that's when you maybe choose not to engage, or if you do, because you have already begun in a manner which deflates the other person, you are in a better position to keep calm, maintain your composure, and can better control the outcome.

People don't normally expect you to 'invite' them to provide evidence for what they believe, because we tend to be too polite to ask or we'd rather not be perceived as challenging them – this is one reason why I have often found myself in 'trouble' down the years – if someone makes a claim or accusation, I ask them to back it up, or provide evidence or account for their claim. And they were often miffed that I would even ask.

One way of minimising debate or discussion is just through simple statements, *let me see if I get this* or *let me see if I understand you correctly, what you're saying is…?* which puts you in control, allows you to manage your response and puts the focus back on the person doing the accusation, rather than you just merely countering what they are saying with a counter-claim and getting drawn into an unnecessary discussion, that as we well know, can escalate very quickly and lead you down paths you've never trodden before.

When responding to someone who has just accused us of something, the mistake we all too often make, and I should know, I have made it more times than I care to remember, is that we immediately react, our backs are up, defences armed and we're ready to 'clever them into submission' with our well-rounded and carefully choreographed replies.

We can endeavour to hold our nerve and remain calm as we address their claims but ultimately it doesn't look pleasant either way, and in the heat of the moment, things are often lost in translation because we mishear or we simply assume to know what the other person is saying, and therefore the need for clarity cannot be underestimated. All it requires is to begin by finding out what the other person really means.

Try to remember that if we begin by defending ourselves, we have already succumbed to their plan or if it's not their plan, at least we are caught in their unintentional trap, where if you rush to defend yourself, they react, and then you react, and they double-down and before you know it, yip, completely escalated! So, try and hold your nerve, breathe before you react, and 'force' the person making the allegation to explain themselves. Put them into the position where they must stand over what they have said, rather than putting them in a position of power where all they are doing is making claims and allegations.

There is a degree of pleasure in 'forcing' someone to explain – they can tend to 'go off on one', or they have to summon the courage to back up their words with evidence, not in a scientific kind of way, but you are making them not only accountable but also challenging them to assume responsibility. It's in these moments, you learn something about that person.

Now, the reality is that if you don't really know the person, or they don't have any major involvement in your life, you can perhaps just choose to ignore them. That adage of 'pick your battles' seems apt, but if you do care about the person or the situation enough to challenge their assertions, then try to remember to seek clarity at the outset. Watching someone struggle to back things up or squirm their way out of it can be a joy.

Or even if they do as you ask, they might find your lack of reaction disconcerting, and choose to be less 'full throttle' in their response, and realise that you have the measure of them, and rather than just simply engage in a 'back and forth', they might curb their own enthusiasm and tailor their language in response to yours.

In the event that when you ask them to explain themselves they keep making claims, keep asking them to explain and back it up by seeking clarification – this will 'force' them to lay out their evidence, but in a worst case scenario, let's say they are right and you have to accept at least a little of what they say, you will have avoided reacting, you will have kept your emotions in control, you will have de-escalated the situation, and you might just be able to persuade them that they have got it wrong.

It's important that you don't readily accept criticism without asking for clarification. So often over the years, I responded by defending myself and assuming I knew what their assumptions were, but in recent times I have made a more active choice, to ask people to explain themselves and put them on the spot so that I don't give power to them.

In a bid to minimise conflict and appear to be willing to accept criticism (in the past, particularly when I was younger, I was always accused of not being able to accept it), I ended up giving too much power to the person doing the accusing. These days I endeavour to ask people to politely explain themselves. Before you begin, always seek clarity so you know exactly what you're dealing with – in the end, even the person attacking you might be thankful you did!

45. Let's put things into perspective

'I'm not getting the vaccine, it's a microchip so they know where we are,' says Jade with no qualification in microchips or medicine, on Facebook, via a smart phone, who uses Google Maps to get to places then tags herself into the location with a selfie, listens to Spotify on said phone while there and sometimes jogs using Strava, gets localized offers from Groupon and Quidco and talks to Alexa without the slightest hint or irony... just convinced she's right and the world's best scientists and the NHS have made up an elaborate plot for most of the year with the sole aim of figuring out what night she goes to bingo and how often she pops into Tesco's Express (where she uses her clubcard and credit card), the list could go on...
Unknown

I firmly believe that one of the reasons there is seemingly so much stress and anxiety about us is that we don't have enough perspective or rather we tend to get things out of perspective, and this affects how we see things, and ultimately our resilience, if we allow those things to wear us down.

Not so long ago I read a book called *F**k It* by John C. Parkin (I highly recommend it as to provide much-needed perspective, it's in my list of recommended reads) – it's quite entertaining and funny to read in parts, not to mention easy to read.

Among the many things he wrote was the following:

I am one person among 6.5 billion people on this earth at the moment. That's one person among 6, 500, 000, 000 people.... And we live on an Earth that is spinning at 67, 000mph through space that is at the centre of our solar system (and our solar system is spinning around the centre of the milky way at 530, 000mph).... If you're in for a good innings you may spend 85 years on Earth. Man has been around for 100, 000 years so you're going to spend 0.00085per cent of man's history living on Earth (which is 4.5 billion years old); if the Earth had been the equivalent of a day (with the Big Bang kicking it all off at midnight), humans didn't turn up until 11.59.58pm. That means we've only been around for the last two seconds.[159]

I find his description truly amazing – simplistic in that he offers a perspective that I for one, never thought about. Of course, I didn't have the information to know this and therefore could not simply comprehend such an idea in the first instance. And that is the crux of much of the discourse that surrounds us these days, and of course the irony, as we have access to all the information we could want and therefore when it comes to having perspective we should have no problem in drawing conclusions, yet we are so prone to focus on that which only serves to support our ideas, opinion, and worldview.

By having the 'right' information it is much easier of course to make decisions or reach conclusions which ultimately helps us consider the challenges we face in the future. For example, by 2050 it's estimated that the population of the planet will be close to ten billion people.

Think about that for a moment, ten billion! I am only one person, yet by the time I reach my 80s, the population of the planet will have increased by around two–three billion. So numerous are we, that we could effectively go around being unnoticed our entire lives, which touches upon another issue but that's for another day.

When I read this piece from Steve Parkin it really did occur to me that we are only here for such a short period of time and in the great scheme of things there's not a lot that matters but of the important things that do matter, we should make the most of them or give them most of our attention whilst we are here.

All too often though, by the time we realise the importance of this we are in middle age, and many of the opportunities we have to do exactly that may have already passed us by. When I look back upon my time raising my kids, both during my time when I was married and then separated and divorced, I look back upon them with a tinge of sadness and a little bit of regret. Not for the things I've done (although there are some things I would do differently) but for time moving so quickly as to have deprived me of the appreciation I now have (in my grandfather days) for what it means to be a parent during my actual parenting days.

I have a great relationship with my children and my grandchildren, but it does go so quickly. Suddenly they are at primary school, then high school, then work or college and so on; then they become parents, and then you find it difficult to remember all the things you did, and how in a blink of the eye you are a parent of more than 30 years and wondering how the hell you got there!

And then you become wiser, more compassionate, kinder, less 'controlling', or protective, have a more informed and relaxed approach to parenting, and then look back upon the time when you needed this, yet hadn't grown or matured enough to parent in the way you respond with your grandchildren. Having perspective is the difference between parenting your own children and those of your grandchildren.

Perspective comes through many things – experience, learning to learn, listening, listening to understand, reading to discover and uncover, being curious, not being absolutist, knowing that there is more to know and so on. Having perspective or making time to do so can feel a little like being on your own, so that when you offer what feels like a sound, informed, rational, and well-thought-out view on something you can feel quite alone.

Another quote from John Parkin's wonderful book which proves that we are not alone of course, that when we feel we are the only one's feeling or thinking something then think again, and it's the ability to have perspective that is essential, and the contributions that the likes of John makes is fundamental to helping us understand. In this case, he is speaking of relationships but the essence of it is profound and something we can all relate too.

> If something hurtful is said, we feel it deeply; If we don't feel heard, we feel like children, if we think we love them more than they do us, we feel pain; if we think they love us more than we love them, we feel guilt; if we get excitement from someone outside the relationship we feel confused, if they get excitement from outside the relationship we feel jealous – if life as we live it is about us and the outside world, then your relationship with a partner is the finest thread of that relationship.[160]

There is no great mysterious process for learning how to have perspective. It is some of those things I mentioned above, curiosity, not being absolutist, discovery, reading, etc. The world we live in now demands this of us, but often it feels we are fighting a losing battle. What are the challenges we now face and how do we respond? Overleaf I offer what I believe are the challenges we face. Having a sense of what these are at least prepares us for the road ahead. They are as follows:

- We know that our youth vanishes, that we and our loved ones will die one day, that whatever we have accumulated can easily be taken away from us, that one day our skills might not be wanted, that a day may come when our love might not be reciprocated
- Anything that means something to us has the potential to cause stress and thus we need to think carefully about the things we consider as important

- In most jobs, if you didn't turn up tomorrow, or the next day, of if you fell ill, the organisation and business would continue and if it came to it, would continue without you

As humans we often get so busy, we forget some of the important things that have come to pass and it's good to be reminded or to even learn about them for the first time.

We are so often focused on creating the future we forget the journey we have travelled and how unique we (actually) are, or at least to this planet in any case, not necessarily in terms of the wider universe, or as some would argue, multiverse.

By taking time to reflect on some elements of our story, I think we can better appreciate what we have the potential for, as well as acknowledge the capacity we possess to make a difference, and where we should really concentrate those efforts on in terms of trying to make a difference.

- **we are a species** – and I use the word species as opposed to race, which is in part to challenge us to appreciate that we are just one of the many species that occupy this comparatively small planet and that we should know and remind ourselves of our place in it
- **we are over seven billion people** – *and it's estimated that by 2050 there will be 9.6 billion of us*[161] (more than a one-third increase)
- **our galaxy is made up of between 200 and 400 billion stars** – *and there are an estimated 100 billion galaxies in our universe*[162]
- **the universe is an estimated 17.5 billion years old, and our planet a relatively young 4.5 billion years** – just think about that, Covid has been with us for 2–3 years – try for a moment to imagine 4.5 billion years
- **we branched off from chimps and bonobos about 6 million years ago** – *our first ancestor appeared about 4.4 million years ago*[163]

- **two million years ago, early humanoids (Homo habilis) first appeared on earth** with a brain capacity of 650–700cc; followed by Homo erectus and Neanderthals and finally Homo sapiens – today our brain capacity is around 1500cc[164]
- **1.2 million years ago, it's estimated that there were 18, 500 homini's on earth,** not humans but homini's, i.e., our descendants... *it's estimated that there have been around 700 billion mutations since*[165]
- **thirty-one per cent of our genes can be found in yeast,** *forty per cent in worms, 50 per cent in fruit flies and all but 1.5% in chimpanzees – we are as it were 98.5% chimpanzee* [166]
- **only in the last 10, 000 years has the world begun to truly transform** dramatically with the development of crops, livestock, villages, cities, global trade, and financial markets
- **human beings are 99.9 per cent identical** – genetically speaking, yet we almost entirely focus on the 0.1% of difference
- **6.4 billion letters make up our DNA** and *we are an estimated 50 to 100 letters different from our parents*[167] – anyone who thinks they are completely free from this should temper that belief with that thought – we are more like our parents than we can possibly imagine
- **microbes make up 80% of all biomass...** *in 1/5 of a teaspoon of sea water, there are a million bacteria (and 10 million viruses)... the human microbiome in our gut, mouth, skin and elsewhere, harbour three thousand kinds of bacteria with 3 billion distinct genes*[168]
- **viruses are champions of DNA mutation...** *A single sneeze propels 40, 000 droplets, each containing up to 200 million individual viruses, across the room exceeding speeds of 200mph*[169]

This is pretty amazing when you take time to think about this but here are a couple of interesting thoughts which increases our perspective on things even further.

- **If you spend half an hour in a regular shopping mall,** you will pass more people than our ancestors saw during their entire lifetime
- **did you know that there almost no examples of Neanderthal cavities?**[170] It's an incredible thought – for all the perceptions in our minds of Neanderthals as violent creatures lacking the capacity to think, at least their teeth were in great shape as compared with humans, which begs the question what the hell have we done (as the apparently intelligent humanoid) since then?

After reading this, how do you feel now? What strikes you about all of this? Do you feel humbled? Are you feeling a little bit smaller now? Are you blown away somewhat by this information? Are you looking at things differently now?

When you start to look at the 'bigger picture' you begin to accrue some very well-earned perspective, and the things that occupy your mind normally, take on a different appearance.

Putting things in perspective is a must!

46. Life's important questions

Thinking is difficult, that's why most people judge.
Carl Jung

I have learned over the years that it's important to know what to ask, i.e., asking the 'right' question and the right kind of question at that. It sounds like stating the obvious, but it isn't obvious, at least not to everyone. Imagine the scenario – your son or daughter, or a friend for that matter must break some news to you, news you won't like, and they must find a way of doing it as comfortably as possible, or at least with as little consequence as possible.

We've all been there, thinking over in our mind endlessly, building up to it, gaining the confidence to broach the subject, and picking the right moment. You break the news, and boom, their response is one of *what the...* variety.

Or they tell you in no uncertain terms what they think, and even though you didn't set out to do what has happened, if their reaction strays beyond what you might reasonably expect as a consequence, then you can easily slide into defensive mode, and rather than trying to break the news as easily as possible, the next thing you know is that you're defending yourself, and highlighting all the bad habits of the other person, and suddenly your relationship is at risk. We've all been there!

Whilst it's hard to not react to certain news, we know that ultimately reacting doesn't tend to help. I'm not of course talking about very serious matters – you couldn't really excuse anyone reacting when they have just discovered something of a quite serious nature. I'm talking more about day-to-day things – you forgot to collect something, you broke something, you told someone to feck off, you lost money and so on, you've changed your mind about something and so on, things like this.

With that in mind, it's important to find questions that get to the crux of the issue or put a different slant on common questions, so, for example, people might ask you 'what's wrong with you?' which is quite broad, but the first question on the list (overleaf) tends to be much more specific and one that is rarely asked. Asking someone *what exactly is bothering you?* challenges an individual to focus on the feeling or feelings that are overwhelming or dominating them. By replacing the word 'wrong' with 'bothering', it removes the sense of blame that is attributed to the word 'wrong' or that they are somehow responsible for their feeling(s) that have emerged.

It gives them more freedom to express what's going on with them and makes it okay to talk about it. It also demonstrates that you are interested in what they have to say, and you have time for them, because if you must listen to exactly what's bothering them, it can be assumed you have time to do so. And quite simply as 'what exactly is bothering you?' is different from the traditional 'what's wrong with you' or even 'what's up?' then this adds a new dynamic and offers greater space to explore what is going on in your mind or how you're feeling inside.

Finding a way to ask the right question, is as important as asking the right question. Any question might not be applicable in every situation depending on who you are talking with and the mood they are in, also the moment, timing, the culture, the environment you are in and how much time you might have to give. Overleaf is my list of 'Life's Important Questions' – the things we really need to ask. The list is certainly not exhaustive and perhaps you can add to it. The essential rule is asking the right question – take time to think about it.

1. What exactly is bothering you/me?
2. What are we assuming?
3. What aren't you telling me?
4. What do you need me to understand?

5. What are the things we/I need to deal with?
6. How am I presenting myself and my ideas?
7. Who is it I really need to engage in conversation with?
8. What did you see first of all, and second, what thoughts come to mind?
9. It's reality for you but is it actually reality?
10. What would it be like just to accept yourself as you are?
11. What are the things that have influenced my life – what has made me the person I am?
12. What are the current vacuums in my life? What are the fundamental gaps?
13. Do we practise so much that we become reckless, so much that we neglect risk?
14. Every journey starts with a step, but can I/you take the first step?
15. What do you need/not to happen to make this work for you?
16. How do we/I get to the point that we don't ask questions structured around the reward of feeling in the right?
17. What will be the one area where you/I can sustain my/your passion and creativity to make a difference?
18. Why do I/we let knocks get to us but more so how do we/I react and what underpins my/our resilience?
19. What is presence and how do you get it?
20. If little children demonstrate the characteristics of clarity, presence, joy, creativity, connection, resilience, etc., why is that so often we/I (as older children, teenagers, and adults) don't?
21. Where do the deep, rich, profound feelings in life come from? Where do they go when you're not aware of them?
22. What would happen if you decided not to treat yourself as a 'thing' to be improved, and instead were open to the possibility that it's your nature to continue learning, growing, and evolving?

23. Can we/I enrich ourselves/myself but in a way that also enables the community around us/me to thrive and prosper?
24. What wouldn't people know about me if I suddenly died tomorrow? What are the things they are likely to say rather than the things you would like them to say?
25. That question you've been asking yourself – why have you framed it that way and not another way? And if you were to pose that question to someone else, how might he or she reframe it?
26. Are we individuals just a continuation of lives that existed before us? Are we merely an extension of behaviours inherited from those who have passed?
27. If you don't like to be labelled, then why do you label others?
28. What is it you can offer me or what is your counter-offer?
29. If you walked away from everyone tomorrow, what would they truly say about you? How would they react?
30. If you had no communication for a week, would you be missed and what might happen?

47. Because you feel it doesn't make it right – feelings do not always equal truth

The truth is still the truth even if no one believes it. A lie is still a lie even if everyone believes it.
Unknown

In recent times, it feels like feelings have made a comeback! End of lesson! See what I did there, I feel like feelings have made a comeback. That suggests that feelings went away, somewhere, like disappeared, perhaps on a holiday, or hibernating. The way the world is perceived now, you could say that feelings have made a comeback, and I guarantee you, no one will even stop to question if that statement even makes sense. Why?

Well, everyone perceives or interprets the statement in accordance with their beliefs or worldview, and immediately fills it with assumptions, such as if you are among friends or colleagues when you say it, if they feel comfortable around you, they are likely to express their opinion based on their belief that you and them both share common ground on the subject and therefore, it is safe to do so.

Think about the statement for a moment – how could feelings possibly go away? Like, everyone is suddenly born without them, or suddenly they all have vanished from the inner workings of the human body? Of course not, like me I suspect that most people understand it as a concept if I can use that word as opposed to a literal statement, the idea that people are much more okay with expressing their feelings than ever before, at least in more liberal democracies.

There's an irony of this which I have already alluded to – young people tend to be more comfortable these days in expressing feelings and we're all encouraged to look after our mental health, and one of the ways of doing that is to talk to someone, to open up, to share, yet when we do so, many are described as 'snowflakes'. Although my observation is that it tends to be white middle-aged men of a certain generation that use this language.

Leaving aside certain countries where there is less tolerance, or an authoritarian government in place, and where the power largely sits in the hands of, if not middle-aged white men, at least middle-aged men of a more conservative hue, that tend to believe in more traditional ways of functioning, i.e., marriage between a man and woman (only), who procreate, and traditional roles where males lead and women raise children, and that there should be no deviation from this.

In more conservative countries, expressing feelings threatens the established norms and conventions about how males and females should behave, and the roles they should assume. So, an effective way to minimise this is to ensure that it doesn't happen and actively discourage it, or it's only allowed in certain situations, bereavement or in major sporting events among others. The last ten years has seen the reaffirming of the tough man image – Trump, Putin, Erdogan, Xi, Assad, Bolsonaro and Duterte among others, and this has coincided with the rise once again of conservatism, populism, nationalism, racism, and fascism.

Right now, this clashes with some of the newer values that have emerged in recent times across liberal democracies, and this is often described in terms of a 'cultural war' where the battle for control of how we live and how we are governed is being played out.

The idea of expressing feelings is not always welcome, although the irony, for example, in the United States, where the rise of the Tea Party, the elevation of Trump, and the re-awakening of populism fuelled often by right-wing conspiracies which is often based on a sense of abandonment felt by many in traditional white working-class areas has given rise to claims that are not based on anything evidential, but rather a set of beliefs based on a feeling, or a range of feelings.

For many of the conservatives that would scoff at the 'snowflake' generation for being too 'touchy-feely' and not being tough enough, the irony that the very thing they are criticising them for, is on a par with the very thing they use to underpin their grievances.

As for the statement of feelings making a comeback, I must confess, I'm someone who is of a scientific mindset as it were, (not to be confused with my being a scientist) – I'm someone who bases beliefs and ideas on evidence.

I used to joke that when I was married that I was Spock, and my ex-wife was Kirk – she was the feelings, and I was logic. And of course, if it is logical, it must be right, because there is evidence to back it up. Right? Well for me this still dominates but of course that is quite a simplistic approach, and as someone that doesn't believe in being absolute either, taking feelings into consideration in any conversation, discussion, or debate, is something I have had to navigate over the years, and not always with success I might add.

My last relationship was with someone who was what I might describe as an empath, and I endeavoured during my time with her to be more empathetic. As it was my last relationship (at the time or writing) you can tell I wasn't 100% successful! But I digress.

As someone who grew up in the '70s, it was at a time that expressing feelings wasn't really the done thing. I don't even think this was simply down to the era I grew up in but also just how I am 'constructed' as a person, i.e., mix of what's in my genes as it were and the environment in which I grew up. Also, growing up in Northern Ireland certainly wasn't a place that encouraged you to express your feelings either.

Both my parents were loving parents, but expressing or articulating feelings wasn't their strong points – this is not a criticism, they were of their generation, a generation of keeping a stiff upper limit, keeping a level head, and even conversations about things of a personal nature weren't really on the agenda either, certainly not with me anyways. We never really went without, and whilst there certainly wasn't a lot of money, the essentials were provided, and both my parents worked hard to ensure our needs were met.

Expressing feelings was never really a feature of life – that was something we had to try and navigate by ourselves. Both my parents grew up in an age when it certainly wasn't common, and so, it could hardly be expected they could teach us, and so my journey of managing feelings and emotions has largely been one that I have had to work out on my own, but of course often in situations that contrasts with others, can sometimes be painful moments, and very uncomfortable at times.

So being a 'Spock' in moments that require sensitivity can be quite a challenge for someone whose natural habitat and kindred spirits are among those that look for logic and rational thought. It's only on becoming a father, and more recently a grandfather, and where all my children became adults themselves, have I really found myself reflecting much more in depth, and having a greater appreciation of what it is to be able to not only articulate my feelings but express them in a way that is comfortable for me and reflects what's going on not only inside my mind but how I actually feel in a given moment.

As the world turns, and our various societies toil with all that constitutes daily life, and individuals endeavour to find a path through what often feels like chaos, we have shifted (at least it feels very much like it in the West as many cultures in the East have no probs with articulating their needs and feelings), from a position of not saying what you feel to being positively encouraged to say how you are feeling, and learning how to take better care of yourself, through all sorts of processes, be that meditation, yoga, and mindfulness among many others.

We have begun to recognise that looking after your mental health is vital, as vital as looking after your physical health, and is indeed on a par with each other, i.e., healthy body, healthy mind kind of thing. We always knew that but only in recent times have we given it greater attention and whilst there is still a reticence, if not a stigma to talk about feelings, whilst in some cultures it is labelled as a sign of weakness, there is a growing acceptance in society about the need to understand our feelings and to care for them just in the way we would if we were taking medicine for a headache or a cold.

With such a shift, we are encouraged to articulate how we feel, to recognise its impact, to tend to it and to move forward, but there is also a risk (of sorts) that it comes to dominate to such an extent, that if people feel something, anything, that is the truth, at least for that person and there's no real examination of whether or not it is indeed the reality, then the risk is that it becomes a false narrative.

Now I recognise that as a bit of a 'Spock' approaching things in the way that I do, I am biased. But I'm also human as well, although clearly not Vulcan, and therefore I also have lots of feelings and emotions, and therefore not immune to being sensitive to all manner of things as well. As someone that can also feel certain things in a particular moment, I also reflect upon whether what I feel is the truth, or merely just a reaction, governed by my mood in a given moment.

When I was married, I look back upon it as a time when I was quite mature, but probably not as emotionally mature as I thought I was, in that I wasn't always the most sensitive person in the world, or that I didn't always get it. For example, I didn't really understand post-natal depression, and so I wasn't always the most supportive husband when needing to be. Likewise in my last relationship, I wasn't always the most 'tuned-in'; I had been single for a long time before this, and so I hadn't really had to consider certain things for quite some time. I'm talking about simple things, but my last partner had certain expectations, and, of course, we had to learn to navigate the journey together.

Looking back over those years and being in relationships where I seemed to always be with a 'Kirk', I learned that ultimately it doesn't make people right or wrong, they are who they are, we are who we are and that's that, but also, feelings do not always equal truth – just because you feel it, does not make it right.

The risk that we face in shifting from a culture of not expressing feelings to one where we are all encouraged to express feelings, and if our feelings translate as 'our truth', can provide an interpretation of experiences not necessarily correct but yet bring credibility to narratives that might not actually be reality.

This has become such a feature in recent years on social media, where I have seen people express all manner of thoughts, feeling and opinion, and when you challenge their thinking or beliefs with facts or evidence, it can very quickly deteriorate into a slugfest.

I have challenged friends, family, and colleagues on social media, for example, especially where memes are the order of the day, and even though people are happy to accept likes and affirmations in the form of comments that support their narrative, as soon as you challenge, they can suddenly 'lose the plot'.

Their assertion is often based on their beliefs which often comes from the feeling they have, and once you challenge this, you're not challenging their view but rather them, because their feeling is tied up in their belief system, which of course is intertwined with and reflects their identity, and of course, their identity is a potent mix of feelings and emotions. And as we all know, we are prone to defending our feelings.

What I have found, very much in my own experience, that even if you present evidence that completely contravenes views expressed by others is how unwilling they are to shift from their established position, even if it is clearly wrong, or at the very least misinformed. It's more important for them to be right than to reflect and accept a new position.

I'd be the first to admit it's not easy to accept when you are wrong but having over the years worked on developing a mindset that gives way to new information when it becomes available and trying not to adopt absolutist positions there are times when I find it a bit of a revelation to be wrong, which probably sounds a bit contradictory.

I try to stay as informed as possible but when I'm wrong, I console myself by viewing it through the lens of *every day is a school day* but more widely look upon it as fulfilling one of my aims in life which is to keep learning, to keep growing, to keep evolving. I find that not everyone shares that approach, and whilst I accept that, it is frustrating, because is our ultimate goal in life not to keep learning?

We seem to occupy an era where feelings are gaining in strength built around a notion that no matter what the reality is, your feelings are your truth and therefore they have equal legitimacy with those of everyone else. This of course is problematic, in that if we base truth merely on feelings, we invite everyone to legitimise any feeling they might have and reject what is reality.

I accept that everyone's feelings reflect where they are in a certain moment, and thus are legitimate, but only legitimate for them, and not necessarily legitimate for all.

Feelings do not always equal truth. We need to relearn that, particularly in twenty-first-century Earth.

48. What people really need

We need to get the idea out of our heads that education is limited to something we do with a book, paper, and pencil.
True Aim

Involved in Youth Work for over 30 years, I graduated with a professional qualification in Youth Work in 1995. I have managed youth organisations, youth projects and delivered a range of youth services to a wide variety of young people, across a multitude of settings and age groups. I have reflected on my experiences, and I have come to a clear conclusion – no matter what tool, methodology, practice or gimmick we develop, there are certain things that people require and look for, but ultimately, what we humans need – at least in this case, young people. Below is what I refer to as the *Forgotten Fundamentals*, or as I affectionately refer to as *The 6 Rs*.

Reception: the need to be heard, that you have a voice...
Young People need to be heard. They have much to say but often cannot find the words to express what it is they are thinking or feeling in a particular moment. Perhaps they do not possess the ability to articulate their feelings or thoughts in ways that truly represent the message they wish or need to convey to those that most need to hear it. Irrespective of this, but more importantly, is that someone is listening, that someone is picking up the message, that there is a reception for the signal emanating from them. We need to be that receiver that picks up the signal, no matter how distant or faint it is.

Recognition: the need to be visible, that you exist...
It's nice to be recognised. I'm not necessarily talking about someone that you know who recognises you and even addresses

251

you by name, but rather that people see you – you are there, you are visible, you are not forgotten, and you have merit in the eyes of the person or people that see or hear you. Everyone needs to be seen – even if someone forgets your name, which of course isn't so nice but just to know that people know you are there, that you are not ignored, overlooked, or forgotten, cannot be underestimated. Just having recognition opens up so many possibilities and provides a way in.

Reassurance: the need to know someone is with you, that someone cares...

If you feel that no one cares, it can be a lonely place, so letting someone know you care is nothing short of reassuring – for some it can be the difference between life and death. It can simply be a 'check-in', a phone call, a message, an e-mail. Humans are vulnerable and susceptible often to their own thoughts and if no one is taking an interest in you, or pays you little or no regard, and doesn't take a moment to 'check-in', then unless you are eternally confident, and able to function without fear, by yourself, then this can be a very lonely existence. Young people need supportive adults in their life, and research has shown that if a young person has even one supportive adult in their life, it can have such a positive impact. Young people are trying to 'find themselves' so to speak and to also learn how to navigate many of life's challenges in their adolescent years and therefore having the reassurance of that one solid person in their life is worth its weight in gold. Of course, every human being, young and old, needs that one supportive person.

Reputation: the need to be 'known for something', that you have value...

It's not (really) possible to go through life without having some sort of purpose – just in the way that you might draw, sing, or write, most need to have something in their lives beyond the usual suspects, i.e., education, work, family, or partner. Every human wants to be known for something – it gives them a sense of purpose, a sense of identity and a sense of worth and a feeling of value, and brings with it recognition, credibility and ultimately, reputation. Everyone needs this – no more so than young people – who often need to feel they have something to give, something to get up for and to live for. Especially in this modern era where everyone is under more pressure 'to perform' more than they have ever been – be that in education, work or through a new additional pressure that is, of course, social media, they need people to find that 'something' gives them purpose and helps them achieve reputation among others.

Reflection: the need to be able to change course, that you can think and feel differently...

Young people are well known for getting themselves stuck in the proverbial corner or taking a position that they feel they can't change or appear unwilling to change, for all sorts of reasons, even sometimes for what seems like ludicrous reasons, where no end of reasoning can persuade them otherwise. As is often the case, people feel they can't change, that they have gone too far, because to do so will appear to be contradictory, hypocritical, or inconsistent.

Young people often grow up learning that they can't (or are not supposed to) hold two differing opinions. They can't 'sit on the fence' or rather can't be 'neutral' or assume an impartial stance, that they have to choose, that it's either/or, one way or the other, this or that, and feel that they can't shift, or rather as is often the case, they can't find the words to articulate a change in position and remain aligned to a position they might not support, or end up becoming stuck, and feel they can't move, even when they might want to.

It's imperative, and the onus is on us as adults, to let young people know it's okay to change, that you can hold two differing opinions, that things don't have to be fixed, but with our encouragement and support they can indeed reflect on the ideas, thoughts, opinions and positions they hold about a whole range of matters and can shift their focus or change their mind. We must ensure that people know it's okay to reflect and reach a different conclusion.

Recourse: the need to know that there is a way back, that you can save face...

Because young people often haven't worked out their position on a whole range of matters, they often take decisions only to discover that it was the wrong one, or that it certainly wasn't one that proved correct or brought them any kind of real benefit. For different reasons, they then feel they must stick with it, often afraid to change their mind because it might appear to be a sign of weakness. Just as it's important that we assure individuals they can change their mind through a process of reflection it's also vital that they can 'find a way back', when the decision they have taken isn't to their benefit, that they can 'save face' and have the confidence and ability to articulate a route back. This perhaps means having the capacity for humility, or to acknowledge when they might have been in the wrong or can reconcile with those they might have been in conflict with.

Equally, and more importantly, it also means that they know that whomever they have been in conflict with can also reciprocate towards them and help them to find a way back. If a young person decides they want to change their mind and articulate as much, they need to know that their efforts will not be rejected or spurned. If they take the risk, they must know they have a way to 'save face' – they need to know we are there for them, that we can help smooth the way, and that we do not judge them, nor use their way back as a means to point out their error(s) or to gain any kind of 'one-upmanship'. Young people need to know there is a way back – they need to know there is recourse – and that it is safe recourse.

49. The more I know, the more I realise I don't know... really!

The greatest obstacle to discovery is not ignorance – it is the illusion of knowledge.
Daniel J. Borstein

It is just impossible to know everything – so don't bother trying. It's nice to be able to engage with people across a variety of subjects if only to feel you can contribute to a conversation which ultimately makes you feel good or at least involved (no one wants not to be able to take part in a conversation, right?) but as I've gotten older I've grown to realise that the more I know, the more I know I don't know or to put it another way, the more I know, the more I realise that there is just so much information 'out there' and therefore forget trying to know it all. It takes up too much energy anyways!

In *Total Rethink,* David McCourt reference's Malcolm Gladwell's book *Outliers,* which explores the '10, 000-Hour Rule'. According to a study by Swedish psychologist Aders Ericsson, Gladwell explains that to become 'great', at anything it takes up to 10, 000 hours of practice. This equates to 416 days, but in working days (8 hours per day) it would amount to practising something every day of the year for almost three and a half years. If you took out leave and public holidays, you're closer to four years of non-stop practice.

I find the secret of succeeding is really to decide on the subjects you want to know about and give that time, energy, and commitment. In other areas, especially when you're in the company of others, just put your hands up and say, 'sorry, don't know' and allow yourself to be okay about that.

This might mean not being part of the conversation and perhaps even to risk becoming bored but better that, I suggest, than just trying to bullshit your way through a conversation – something about still waters running deep whilst shallow waters making lots of noise!

I find life, Earth, the planets, stars and the whole universe or even multi-verse completely fascinating, to the point that at times I just sit in awe and wonder. There are moments when I just stop and look around me and think about the things in front of me and how it came to be.

Even something like a car that we take so much for granted these days, i.e., how all the things connect and work in tandem to get the car up and running and keep moving – of course it didn't happen overnight, but it still is an amazing feat of engineering when you just take a moment to think about it.

Equally, there are times when I just sit on the doorstep at the back of my house and watch the squirrels that emerge from the trees behind my house as they forage for food; or all the birds that have made the trees their home, and I just wonder how as creatures they came to be, and all those that came before them, how they evolved, how they become their own distinct species.

With so much information at our disposal, on one hand there's probably a need inherent among us to know 'stuff' or at least feel we can make an active contribution to discourse when called upon, whilst on the other, we are overwhelmed with all the information that is available and find it hard not only to make a decision but to also feel comfortable about sources we can trust.

Maintaining an interest in the likes of current affairs and history, or having an expertise in a chosen subject, enables you to contribute to conversation where it finds you. As we have seen with the emergence and growth of mis- and disinformation, and alongside conspiracy theories, this has led people to reach their own poorly researched and ill-informed narratives, much of which is based on the opinions and beliefs of those that are the least qualified to draw conclusions.

This only serves to nurture a growing inability to interpret information effectively therefore rendering an individual's capacity to make meaningful judgements or draw reasonable conclusions.

The result of this is what has become more commonly known as the 'Dunning-Kruger' effect, which ironically, is a cognitive bias where those with limited knowledge or competence in a particular subject overestimate their own knowledge or competence in that subject.

Once an individual over-estimates their ability about any subject, there is a tendency to over-estimate their ability on a range of subjects and where they are confident in their own assertions, it often appears as arrogant to others, and with that they tend to lack humility as they 'double down' on their ideas and can't bring themselves to review or reflect upon their opinion.

The likelihood of their ever reaching a point where they might say *the more I know, the more I realise I don't know* is limited because, of course, they believe they already know and therefore no need to reflect or review. I'm sure you can already think of people like this.

The point of it all, and of course of this lesson is that I don't really know, I can't know and sometimes it's not necessary to know; it is sometimes more important to just be content that all of it exists at all, and just enjoy the awe and wonder of the world in its many forms.

Even if you are confident in your own beliefs and have the courage of conviction when expressing an opinion, it's always important to remember the principle of *every day is a school day* and there is much to learn.

Ultimately, I can only speak for myself, but all I know is that the more I know, the less I know.

50. (My) Assumptions about the world and the society we live in

Look into your own heart, discover what it is that gives you pain, then refuse under any circumstances to inflict that pain on anybody else.
Karen Armstrong

Now I should add a caveat to this lesson and say that the assumptions I make do not mean we should just accept what I write below because if you have the time, energy, and resources, by all means do your own research and speculating.

These assumptions are more about not getting angry about how things are which in turn allows us to channel energy into creating change rather than reacting.

So here are (just some of) my assumptions about the world we live in.

- Parliamentary politics is fundamentally corrupt (that doesn't necessarily mean politicians are fiddling expenses or providing 'jobs for the boys' although we know that goes on) so let's just get over it and let the fuckers get on with it, or get up and do something about it
- Ultimately funding is skewed towards particular areas of work be that at the whim of a politician or personality of some kind
- No matter what you will do, people will talk about you anyway so don't sweat it
- Don't be reliant on others – be open to support others but ultimately take care of yourself – that way you're the only one who can fuck it up and thus you won't be angry at anyone else

- Commerce/business and similar have made an industry out of fear
- 'We' have built an existence out of complication as opposed to simplicity – it's time to approach things in a more simplistic fashion
- 'We' have created an industry of language in almost every industry in order to cause confusion and elitism so that the ignorance of the majority can be exploited. Need is then created, fear of not servicing that need is instilled in populations, and panic and crisis ensues. Those who have created the language then respond through their being 'interested' or 'concerned' and (then just happen to be) available to provide a perceived and much needed service to respond to the need.
- To those in power, don't tell me not to be political when all around me is political and almost every decision I make is in response to policy decisions of those in authority and government

References

Lesson 1

1. *Evolving Ourselves: How Unnatural Selection Is Changing Life on Earth*, Enriquez J. and Gullans S., One World, 2015

Lesson 2

2. *Team Human*, Douglas Ruskhoff, W.W. Norton & Company, 2019
3. *What should we be worried about? Real Scenarios That Keep Scientists Up at Night* Technology may endanger democracy (Haim Harari), Brockman J., Harper Perennial, 2014
4. *More Human: Designing a World Where People Come First*, Hilton S., W H Allen, 2015
5. *Age of Anger*, Mishra P., Penguin, 2018
6. *Clarity, Clear Mind, Better Performance, Bigger Results*, Smart J., Capstone, 2013
7. *Nervous States: How Feeling Took Over the World*, Davies W., Jonathan Cape, 2018
8. *Nervous States: How Feeling Took Over the World*, Davies W., Jonathan Cape, 2018

Lesson 3

9. *This will make you smarter: New Scientific Concepts to Improve Your Thinking*, (Randomness, Charles Seife), Brockman J., Black Swan, 2012
10. *The Growth Delusion: The Wealth and Well-Being of Nations*, Pilling D., Bloomsbury, 2018
11. *Know This: Today's Most Interesting and Important Scientific Ideas, Discoveries and Developments*, Brockman J., Harper Perennial, 2017

Lesson 5

12. *Beyond Human Nature*, Prinz J.J., W.W.Norton Company, 2012
13. *Quiet: The Power of Introverts in a World That Can't Stop Talking*, Cain S., Penguin Books, 2013
14. *This will make you smarter: New Scientific Concepts to Improve Your Thinking* (The Mediocrity Principle, Meyers PZ), Brockman J., Black Swan, 2012

Lesson 7

15. *Clarity, Clear Mind, Better Performance, Bigger Results*, Smart J., Capstone, 2013
16. *The Compassionate Mind*, Gilbert P., Constable, 2013
17. *Out of the Wreckage: A New Politics for an Age of Crisis*, Monbiot G., Verso, 2017

Lesson 9

18. *The Compassionate Mind*, Paul Gilbert, Constable, 2013

Lesson 10

19. *Beyond Human Nature*, Prinz J.J., W.W. Norton Company, 2012
20. *This will make you smarter: New Scientific Concepts to Improve Your Thinking* (Dualities, Amanda Gelter), Brockman J., Black Swan, 2012
21. *Serious Creativity: How to be creative under pressure and turn ideas into action*, De Bono E., Penguin Random House UK, 199
22. Participle –Wikipedia

Lesson 11

23. *This will make you smarter: New Scientific Concepts to Improve Your Thinking* (Microbes run the world, Stewart Brand), Brockman J., Black Swan 2012

24. *Nervous States: How Feeling Took Over the World*, Davies W., Jonathan Cape, 2018

Lesson 12
25. *Thinking Fast and Slow*, Khaneman D., Penguin Books, 2011
26. *You Are Not So Smart, Why Your Memory Is Mostly Fiction, Why You Have Too*
27. *Many Friends on Facebook and 46 Other Ways You are Deluding Yourself*, Mc Rainey D., One World, 2012

Lesson 13
28. *The Compassionate Mind*, Gilbert P., Constable, 2013
29. *Age of Anger*, Mishra P., Penguin, 2018

Lesson 14
30. *Know this* (The continually new you, Kosslyn S.M.), Brockman J., Harper Perennial, 2017
31. *Diversify – How to challenge inequality and why we should*, Sarpong J., Harper Collins, 2019

Lesson 15
32. *The Organised Mind: Thinking Straight in the Age of Information Overload*, Levitin D.J., Viking, 2014
33. *The Great Acceleration: How the World Is Getting Faster, Faster*, Colville R., Bloomsbury Publishing, 2016
34. *The Organised Mind: Thinking Straight in the Age of Information Overload*, Levitin D.J., Viking, 2014
35. *The Coddling of the American Mind*, Lukianoff G. and Haidt J., Allen Lane, 2018

Lesson 16
36. *Team Human*, Rushkoff D., W.W. Norton & Company, 2019
37. *Utopia for Realists and How We Got There*, Bregman R., Bloomsbury, 2018

38. *#newpower: Why outsiders are winning, institutions are failing, and how the rest of us can keep up in the age of mass participation,* Timms H. & Jeremy Heimans J., Picador, 2019

39. *The Organised Mind: Thinking Straight in the Age of Information Overload,* Levitin D.J., Viking 2014

Lesson 17

40. *The Organised Mind: Thinking Straight in the Age of Information Overload,* Levitin D.J., Viking 2014

41. *What should we be worried about?* (Is the new public sphere... public? Andre Lih), Brockman J., Harper Perennial, 2014

42. *What should we be worried about? Real Scenarios That Keep Scientists Up at Night* (Present-ism Noga Arikha), Brockman J., Harper Perennial, 2014

43. *All I Ever Wanted Was a One-Trick Pony: Our devices do way too much—and not always on our behalf,* Tufekci Z., www.wired.com, 24 September 2019

44. *What should we be worried about? Real Scenarios That Keep Scientists Up at Night* (The Patience Deficit, Nicholas G. Carr), Brockman J., Harper Perennial, 2014

45. *What should we be worried about? Real Scenarios That Keep Scientists Up at Night* (Illusions of understanding and the loss of intellectual humility, Tania Lombrozo), Brockman J., Harper Perennial, 2014

46. *Know This:* (Broke people ignoring $20 bills on the sidewalk, Michael Vassar), Brockman J., Harper Perennial, 2017

47. *Who can you trust? How Technology Brought Us Together and Why It Could Drive Us Apart,* Botsman R., Penguin Business, 2018

48. *This will make you smarter, New Scientific Concepts to Improve Your Thinking,* (KeyFabe, Eric Weinstein), Brockman J., Black Swan, 2012

49. *Utopia for Realists and How We Got There,* Bregman R., Bloomsbury, 2018

Lesson 18

50. *Quiet: The Power of Introverts in a World That Can't Stop Talking, Cain S.,* Penguin 2012

51. *This will make you smarter: New Scientific Concepts to Improve Your Thinking,* (The Double-Blind Control Experiment, Richard Dawkins), Brockman J., Black Swan, 2012

Lesson 19

52. *You Are Not So Smart: Why Your Memory Is Mostly Fiction, Why You Have Too Many Friends on Facebook and 46 Other Ways You are Deluding Yourself,* David Mc Rainey D., One World, 2012

Lesson 20

53. *The Chimp Paradox: The Mind Management Programme for Confidence, Success and Happiness,* Prof Peters S., Vermillion London, 2012

Lesson 21

54. *The Organised Mind: Thinking Straight in the Age of Information Overload,* Levitin D.J., Viking 2014

55. *The Art of Thinking Clearly,* Dobelli R., Sceptre, 2013

56. *Not Knowing: The Art of Turning Uncertainty into Opportunity,* D'Souza S., and Renner D., LID Publishing Ltd, 2016

Lesson 22

57. *I think you'll find it's more complicated than that,* Goldacre B., Fourth Estate, 2015

58. *What we should be worried about? Real Scenarios That Keep Scientists Up at Night* (Illusions of understanding and the loss of intellectual humility, Tania Lombrozo), Brockman J., Harper Perennial, 2014

59. *The Idiot Brain: A Neuroscientist Explains What Your Head Is Really Up To,* Burnett D., Guardian Books, 2016

Lesson 27

60. *The Spirit Level: Why Equality Is Better for Everyone*, Wilkinson R., and Pickett K, Penguin Books, 2010
61. *Quiet: The Power of Introverts in a World That Can't Stop Talking*, Cain S., Penguin Books, 2012
62. *What should we be worried about? Real Scenarios That Keep Scientists Up at Night* (What is a good life, David Christian), Brockman J., Harper Perennial, 2014
63. *What should we be worried about? Real Scenarios That Keep Scientists Up at Night* (Objects of Desire, Sherry Turkle), Brockman J., Harper Perennial, 2014

Lesson 28

64. *Clarity, Clear Mind, Better Performance, Bigger Results*, Smart J., Captsone 2013

Lesson 31

65. *Diversify – How to challenge inequality and why we should*, Sarpong J., Harper Collins, 2019
66. *The Spirit Level: Why Equality Is Better for Everyone*, Wilkinson R., and Pickett K, Penguin Books, 2010
67. *Diversify – How to challenge inequality and why we should*, Sarpong J., Harper Collins, 2019
68. *What should we be worried about? Real Scenarios That Keep Scientists Up at Night* (Are we homogenizing the global view of a normal mind? Murali Doraiswamy P.), Brockman J., Harper Perennial, 2014
69. *Age of Anger*, Mishra P., Penguin, 2018
70. *Post Capitalism: A Guide to Our Future*, Mason P., Penguin Books, 2016
71. *#newpower: Why outsiders are winning, institutions are failing, and how the rest of us can keep up in the age of mass participation*, Timms H., & Heimans J., Picador, 2019

72. *Nervous States: How Feeling Took Over the World*, Davies W., Jonathan Cape, 2018

73. *Evolving Ourselves*, Enriquez J., and Gullans S., Oneworld Publications, 2015

74. *The Great Acceleration: How the World Is Getting Faster, Faster*, Colville R., Bloomsbury Publishing, 2016

75. *Out of the Wreckage:, A New Politics for an Age of Crisis*, Monbiot G., Verso, 2017

76. *Team Human*, Ruskhoff D., W.W. Norton & Company, 2019

77. *Evolving Ourselves*, Enriquez J., and Gullans S., Oneworld Publications, 2015

78. *The Great Acceleration: How the World Is Getting Faster, Faster*, Colville R., Bloomsbury Publishing, 2016

79. *Laugh Your Way to Happiness: Using the Science of Laughter for Total Well Being*, Lyle L., Watkins Publishing Limited, 2014

80. *Secrets of Happy People*, Matt Avery M., Teach Yourself, 2014

81. *Beyond Human Nature*, Prinz J.J., W.W. Norton Company, 2012

82. *Utopia for Realists and How We Got There*, Bregman R., Bloomsbury, 2018

83. *Out of the Wreckage: A New Politics for an Age of Crisis*, Monbiot G., Verso, 2017

84. *What should we be worried about? Real Scenarios That Keep Scientists Up at Night* (The Patience Deficit, Nicholas G. Carr), Brockman J., Harper Perennial, 2014

85. Sally Dickenson and Margaret Kemeny, Psychologists, University of California collected findings from 208 reports of experiments and said that the 'social self' which we try to defend 'reflects one's esteem and status, and is largely based on others' perceptions of one's worth'.

86. *The Coddling of the American Mind*, Lukianoff G., and Haidt J., Allen Lane, 2018

87. Jean Twenge, a psychologist at San Diego State University found 269 broadly comparable studies measuring anxiety levels in the USA at various times between 1952 and 1993

88. Jean Twenge presented graphs showing that digital media use and mental health problems are correlated – they rose together in recent years

89. According to the non-profit organization Common Sense Media, teens spend on average nine hours per day on screens, and eight- to twelve-year-olds spend about six hours

90. *This will make you smarter: New Scientific Concepts to Improve Your Thinking, Hunting for Root Cause: The Human Black Box*, Eric Topol, Brockman J., Black Swan, 2012

91. *This will make you smarter: New Scientific Concepts to Improve Your Thinking*, Brockman J., Black Swan, 2012

92. How Much Data Is Created Every Day in 2021? [You'll be shocked!] (techjury.net)

93. 'Dweck, distinguishes between two mind sets. A fixed mind set [and a] growth mind set... Dweck agrees that those who have a fixed mind set need to constantly prove themselves and confirm to themselves and others their capability.'

94. 'They have missed out on many of the challenges, negative experiences, and minor risks that help children develop into strong, competent, and independent adults... no opportunity to develop their antifragility.'

95. 'A study by the University of Michigan comparing results from 1981 with 1997 found that play among kids under 13 went down 16% and much of the play had shifted to indoor activities, often involving a computer and no other children.'

96. *The Organised Mind: Thinking Straight in the Age of Information Overload*, Levitin D.J., Viking 2014

97. *More Human: Designing a World Where People Come First*, Hilton S., W. H. Allen, 2015

Lesson 33

98. *Evolving Ourselves*, Enriquez J., and Gullans S., Oneworld Publications, 2015
99. *The Great Acceleration: How the World Is Getting Faster, Faster*, Colville R., Bloomsbury Publishing, 2016
100. *What should we be worried about? Real Scenarios That keep Scientists Up at Night* (Worrying about stupid, Roger Schank), Brockman J., Harper Perennial, 2014
101. *What should we be worried about? Real Scenarios That keep Scientists Up at Night* (A world of cascading crises, Peter Schwartz), Brockman J., Harper Perennial, 2014
102. *This will make you smarter: New Scientific Concepts to Improve Your Thinking*, Risk Literacy, Gerd Gigevenzer, Brockman J., Black Swan, 2012

Lesson 34

103. *Know This: Today's Most Interesting and Important Scientific Ideas, Discoveries and Developments* (The universe is infinite, Rudy Rucker), Brockman J., Harper Perennial, 2017
104. *Team Human*, Ruskhoff D., W.W. Norton & Company, 2019

Lesson 36

105. Humour, http://www.pbs.org/thisemotionallife/topic/humor/humor
106. *Redeeming laughter: the comic dimension of human experience*, Berger P., De Gruyter, 1997
107. *Ideas that Changed the World*, Arnesto Fernandez F., DK, 2003
108. Laughter Is the Best Medicine, http://www.helpguide.org/life/humor_laughter_health.htm
109. http://www.pbs.org/thisemotionallife/topic/humor/humor
110. *The pursuit of happiness: your inalienable right*, Phillips S. Dr., http://www.pbs.org/thisemotionallife/blogs/pursuit-happiness-your-inalienable-right

111. 21 hours: Why a shorter working week can help us all to flourish in the 21st century, nef (the new economics foundation), 21 hours | New Economics Foundation
112. *Laugh your way to Happiness*, Lesley Lyle L., Watkins Publishing, 2014
113. *Laugh your way to Happiness*, Lesley Lyle L., Watkins Publishing, 2014
114. *Comedy: a geographic and historical guide*, Charney, M. 2005, Praeger
115. *Laughter Is the Best Medicine*, http://www.helpguide.org/life/humor_laughter_health.htm
116. https://www.inc.com/kevin-daum/8-ways-using-humor-will-make-you-a-betterleader.html
117. 9 Ways Humor Heals – The Second Pilgrimage (thereseborchard.com)
118. Humour & Resilience, http://www.pbs.org/thisemotionallife/topic/humor/humor-and resilience
119. *Laughing our Way to Peace or War: Humour and Peacebuilding*, Zelizer C., 2010
120. *Cultivating Peace*, James O'Dea J., Shift Books, 2012
121. https://psychology.fandom.com/wiki/Gelotology
122. https://elitecareemergency.com/well-being/is-laughter-the-best-medicine/
123. *The science of comedy: can humour make the world a better place?* Jeffries S., The Guardian, Tuesday 11 February 2014 http://www.theguardian.com/stage/2014/feb/11/science-comedy-academics-social

Lesson 37

124. *What should we be worried about? Real Scenarios That Keep Scientists Up at Night* (Armageddon, Timothy Taylor), Brockman J., Harper Perennial, 2014

Lesson 38

125. *The Rules of Life: A Personal Code for living a better, happier, more successful kind of life*, Templar R., Pearson, 2012
126. *Secrets of Happy People*, Avery M., Teach Yourself, 2014
127. *Stuffocation, Living More with Less*, Wallman J., Penguin Books, 2015
128. *The Growth Delusion: The Wealth and Well-Being of Nations*, David Pilling D, Bloomsbury Publishing, 2019
129. *The Art of Thinking Clearly*, Dobelli R., Sceptre, 2013

Lesson 40

130. *You Are Not So Smart: Why Your Memory Is Mostly Fiction, Why You Have Too Many Friends on Facebook and 46 Other Ways You are Deluding Yourself*, Mc Rainey D., One World, 2012
131. *You Are Not So Smart: Why Your Memory is Mostly Fiction, Why You Have Too Many Friends on Facebook and 46 Other Ways You are Deluding Yourself*, Mc Rainey D., One World, 2012

Lesson 41

132. *Nervous States: How Feeling Took Over the World*, Davies W., Jonathon Cape, 2018
133. *Out of the Wreckage: A New Politics for an Age of Crisis*, Monbiot G., Verso, 2017
134. *Who can you trust? How Technology Brought Us Together and Why It Could Drive Us Apart*, Botsman R., Penguin Business, 2018
135. *Team Human*, Rushkoff D., W.W. Norton & Company, 2019
136. *Age of Anger*, Mishra P., Penguin, 2018
137. *Team Human*, Rushkoff D., W.W. Norton & Company, 2019
138. *#newpower: Why outsiders are winning, institutions are failing, and how the rest of us can keep up in the age of mass participation*, Timms H. & Heimans J., Picador, 2019

139. *The Idiot Brain: A Neuroscientist Explains What Your Head Is Really Up To*, Burnett D., Guardian Books, 2016
140. *Out of the Wreckage: A New Politics for an Age of Crisis*, Monbiot G., Verso, 2017
141. *You Are Not So Smart: Why Your Memory Is Mostly Fiction, Why You Have Too Many Friends on Facebook and 46 Other Ways You are Deluding Yourself*, Mc Rainey D., One World, 2012
142. *Total Rethink: Why Entrepreneurs Should Act Like Revolutionaries*, Mc Court D., Red Door, 2018
143. *The Compassionate Mind*, Paul Gilbert P., Constable, 2013
144. *Not Knowing: The Art of Turning Uncertainty into Opportunity*, D'Souza S., Renner D., LID Publishing Ltd, 2016

Lesson 42
145. *The Great Acceleration: How the World Is Getting Faster, Faster*, Colville R., Bloomsbury Publishing, 2016
146. *The Great Acceleration: How the World is Getting Faster, Faster*, Colville R., Bloomsbury Publishing, 2016
147. *More Human: Designing a World Where People Come First*, Hilton S., and Allen W.H., 2015
148. *Utopia for Realists and How We Got There*, Bregman R., Bloomsbury, 2018
149. *The Great Acceleration: How the World Is Getting Faster, Faster*, Colville R., Bloomsbury Publishing, 2016
150. *Evolving Ourselves*, Enriquez J. and Gullans S., Oneworld Publications, 2015
151. *More Human: Designing a World Where People Come First*, Hilton S., and Allen W.H., 2015
152. *What should we be worried about? Real Scenarios That Keep Scientists Up at Night* (A world without growth? Satyajit Das), Brockman J., Harper Perennial, 2014
153. *Nervous States: How Feeling Took Over the World*, William Davies W., Jonathon Cape J, 2018

154. *The Great Acceleration: How the World Is Getting Faster, Faster*, Colville R., Bloomsbury Publishing, 2016
155. *The Growth Delusion: The Wealth and Well-Being of Nations*, Pilling D., Bloomsbury Publishing, 2019
156. *Who can you trust? How Technology Brought Us Together and Why It Could Drive Us Apart*, Botsman R., Penguin Business, 2018
157. *Nervous States: How Feeling Took Over the World*, William Davies W., Jonathon Cape, 2018
158. *Team Human*, Douglas Ruskhoff D., W.W. Norton & Company, 2019

Lesson 45

159. *F**k It: The ultimate spiritual way*, John C. Parkin, J.C., Hay House, 2011
160. *F**k It: The ultimate spiritual way*, John C. Parkin, J.C., Hay House, 2011
161. *Post Capitalism: A Guide to Our Future*, Mason P., Penguin Books, 2016
162. *Know This: Today's Most Interesting and Important Scientific Ideas, Discoveries and Developments* (Extraterrestrials don't land on earth! David Christian), Brockman J., Harper Perennial, 2017;
163. *Evolving Ourselves*, Juan Enriquez J., and Gullans S., Oneworld Publications, 2015
164. *Compassionate Mind*, Gilbert P., Constable, 2013
165. *Evolving Ourselves*, Enriquez J., and Gullans S., Oneworld Publications, 2015
166. *Beyond Human Nature*, Jesse J. Prinz J.J., W.W. Norton Company, 2012
167. *Evolving Ourselves:* Enriquez and Steve Gullans, Oneworld Publications, 2015

168. *This will make you smarter: New Scientific Concepts to Improve Your Thinking* (Microbes run the world, Stewart Brand), Brockman J., Transworld Publishers, 2012

169.*Evolving Ourselves*, Enriquez J., and Gullans S., Oneworld Publications, 2015

170. *Evolving Ourselves*, Enriquez J., and Gullans S., Oneworld Publications, 2015

IFF
BOOKS

ACADEMIC AND SPECIALIST

Iff Books publishes non-fiction. It aims to work with authors
and titles that augment our understanding of the human
condition, society and civilisation, and the world or universe
in which we live. If you have enjoyed this book, why not tell
other readers by posting a review on your preferred book site.
Recent bestsellers from Iff Books are:

Why Materialism Is Baloney
How true skeptics know there is no death and fathom answers
to life, the universe, and everything
Bernardo Kastrup
A hard-nosed, logical, and skeptic non-materialist
metaphysics, according to which the body is in mind, not
mind in the body.
Paperback: 978-1-78279-362-5 ebook: 978-1-78279-361-8

The Fall
Steve Taylor
The Fall discusses human achievement versus the issues of war,
patriarchy and social inequality.
Paperback: 978-1-78535-804-3 ebook: 978-1-78535-805-0

Brief Peeks Beyond
Critical essays on metaphysics, neuroscience, free will,
skepticism and culture
Bernardo Kastrup
An incisive, original, compelling alternative to current
mainstream cultural views and assumptions.
Paperback: 978-1-78535-018-4 ebook: 978-1-78535-019-1

Framespotting
Changing how you look at things changes how you see them
Laurence & Alison Matthews
A punchy, upbeat guide to framespotting. Spot deceptions
and hidden assumptions; swap growth for growing up. See
and be free.
Paperback: 978-1-78279-689-3 ebook: 978-1-78279-822-4

Is There an Afterlife?
David Fontana
Is there an Afterlife? If so what is it like? How do Western
ideas of the afterlife compare with Eastern? David Fontana
presents the historical and contemporary evidence for
survival of physical death.
Paperback: 978-1-90381-690-5

Nothing Matters
a book about nothing
Ronald Green
Thinking about Nothing opens the world to everything by
illuminating new angles to old problems and stimulating new
ways of thinking.
Paperback: 978-1-84694-707-0 ebook: 978-1-78099-016-3

Panpsychism
The Philosophy of the Sensuous Cosmos
Peter Ells
Are free will and mind chimeras? This book, anti-materialistic
but respecting science, answers: No! Mind is foundational to
all existence.
Paperback: 978-1-84694-505-2 ebook: 978-1-78099-018-7

Punk Science
Inside the Mind of God
Manjir Samanta-Laughton
Many have experienced unexplainable phenomena; God,
psychic abilities, extraordinary healing and angelic encounters.
Can cutting-edge science actually explain phenomena
previously thought of as 'paranormal'?
Paperback: 978-1-90504-793-2

The Vagabond Spirit of Poetry
Edward Clarke
Spend time with the wisest poets of the modern age and of the
past, and let Edward Clarke remind you of the importance of
poetry in our industrialized world.
Paperback: 978-1-78279-370-0 ebook: 978-1-78279-369-4

Readers of ebooks can buy or view any of these bestsellers by
clicking on the live link in the title. Most titles are published
in paperback and as an ebook. Paperbacks are available in
traditional bookshops. Both print and ebook formats are
available online. Find more titles and sign up to our readers'
newslett er at http://www.johnhuntpublishing.com/non-fiction
Follow us on Facebook at
https://www.facebook.com/JHPNonFiction
and Twitter at https://twitter.com/JHPNonFiction